Work Experience, Placements and Internships

Work Experience, Placements and Internships

Steve Rook

 macmillan education   palgrave

First published 2016 by PALGRAVE

Palgrave in the UK is an imprint of Macmillan Publishers Limited, registered in England, company number 785998, of 4 Crinan Street, London, N1 9XW.

Palgrave Macmillan in the US is a division of St Martin's Press LLC, 175 Fifth Avenue, New York, NY 10010.

Palgrave is a global imprint of the above companies and is represented throughout the world.

Palgrave® and Macmillan® are registered trademarks in the United States, the United Kingdom, Europe and other countries.

ISBN 978–1–137–46201–5 paperback

This book is printed on paper suitable for recycling and made from fully managed and sustained forest sources. Logging, pulping and manufacturing processes are expected to conform to the environmental regulations of the country of origin.

A catalogue record for this book is available from the British Library.

A catalog record for this book is available from the Library of Congress.

Printed in China

Contents

Preface

I have been encouraged to write this book because of the fantastic feedback I've received on my Graduate Career Guidebook which has been out for a few years now and is proving to be a great success.

Whilst touring the country over the last couple of years talking to students, graduates, academics, employers and careers advisers, I have found that employment experience continues to grow in importance in the recruitment process. I'm not surprised by this because experience is such a great way for employers to 'try before they buy'. However, I'm conscious that the need to build up impressive CVs before even applying for graduate jobs puts an even greater burden on students and graduates. You have to take such focused control of your futures at a time when it's hard enough dealing with the present! Therefore, I've written a guide, which, I hope, will help everyone, at every stage, take a step back and make the most of your journeys into the big bad world!

Enjoy the drive. Some roads will be dull and confusing, some damn right scary but, others will be full of sunshine and promise and you'll develop great energy and enjoyment from being the master of your own destiny. Feel free to email me any time at steventhomasrook@yahoo.co.uk.

Steve Rook

Acknowledgements

My main supporters in this guide have been my lovely wife, Susan, and supportive and inspiring mentor and editor, Suzannah Burywood. I don't find writing easy because I have an overwhelming drive to present my ideas, advice and guidance in the most accessible and useful way I can find. So, some days go on and on, and I rely on these dual literary sentinels to keep me on track!

I also want to say a big thanks to all the academics and advisers who have welcomed me to talk to their students from Swansea to Preston. I massively enjoy these visits! If you want me to inspire students at your university, just drop me a line at steventhomasrook@yahoo.co.uk. Off to Ireland next week to see the students at Institiúid Teicneolaíochta Dhún Dealgan (and visit a few bars in Temple Bar!).

Introduction: Why you need this book

Contents

You only live once

As a student or graduate in today's recruitment market you have an incredible range of career options. However, more than ever before, it's crucial to take control of your own destiny. This employability journey means you have to trawl through all your choices, find the best path and develop the exact skills you need to move forward. This also means you need experience, and lots of it.

This book takes you through this skill development process, from day 1 at university right through to graduation. This journey is illustrated below.

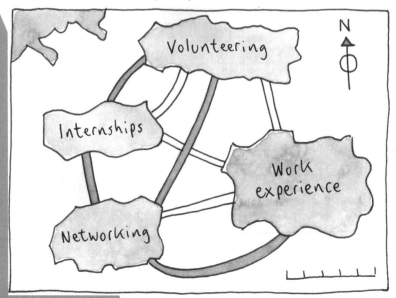

What's covered?

Throughout this guide, the experience journey has been systematically and carefully broken up into its individual tasks so that you can focus on one issue at a time, at your own leisure. However, of course, life is rarely so simple. Therefore, the book has also been designed to help you move freely and easily from one issue to another. For example, if you're writing your CV for a meeting your mum has arranged with a local entrepreneur, you could find yourself jumping back and forth between the following chapters:

- Managing your networks and social media (Chapter 3)
- University, societies and volunteering (Chapter 4)
- Applications and interviews (Chapter 9).

Who it's for

This book is for students and graduates at every stage in their career journeys. You'll find something here, whether you're an overachieving first-year student ready to take up formal experience and internships or a graduate just starting out on your experience trail. The good news is, it's never too early or too late to get stuck in.

Information, advice and guidance

Yes, with this book, you get all three! Where information is defined as data and intelligence, advice involves instruction on how to move forward, and guidance is more personalised feedback to help you take control.

Guidance is achieved through a range of coaching methodologies – in particular, the regular use of self-assessment activities in combination with pointers as to how you can progress according to your specific answers. This is exemplified in the exercise below and the following box labelled 'Reflecting on your answer'. Try this activity right now to see how a bit of reflection can go a long way! You can complete all the exercises in the book at www.plagravecareerskills.com or download them as required.

Self-assessment: Where do you want to start?

In the table below:

1　Identify four distinct things you're keen to research about work experience and internships.
2　Place them in the order in which you think they should be tackled.
3　Find the page where you want to start.

Four aspects of work experience and internships you want to research		
The four aspects	The order in which they should be tackled	The page where you want to start
1.		
2.		
3.		
4.		

Reflecting on your answers:

- If you just quickly looked over this exercise, do you need to give it more attention?
- If you've jumped straight to researching internships or graduate jobs, have you overlooked the foundations?
- If you're still looking at basic experience when you already have plenty – are you being brave enough to move on?

You get out what you put in

Hard graft and personal reflection are essential elements to successful work experience. This book can't do the work for you, but it will assist with the overall management of your journey. You will gain most from each topic if you carefully digest each learning point, read more widely and personally engage with the exercises. This will put you in the driving seat.

Why a book is best

The book is dead – long live the book! All new inventions supposedly herald the death of old technologies, but this book perfectly complements its younger and newer competitors for the following reasons:

- You can rely on its quality, authority and advice.
- It has room for numerous examples and exercises.
- The contents are not biased towards the commercial interests of the publisher, so it focuses on every sector, not just the blue-chip employers.
- There are no adverts.
- It provides usable personal guidance as well as information and advice.
- It has a uniform structure which easily enables quick reference across a broad range of topics.
- It builds up knowledge in a logical, cumulative way.
- It can be used as a universal directory/arachniography of useful websites and social networks at a time when the World Wide Web is buckling under the weight of utter dross.

The companion website

For students

You'll find all the exercises in the book plus additional activities, up-to-date statistics and a wealth of extra links on the companion website at www.palgravecareerskills.com.

For academics/ advisers and teachers

www.palgravecareerskills.com also contains various resources for teachers including:

- PowerPoint presentations of each of the topics addressed throughout this guide.
- Suggestions for group activities on each topic.
- Sample module outlines for work experience modules.
- Ideas for assessments.

Steve Rook often tours the UK delivering energetic and inspiring workshops for students on all the employability and enterprise issues covered in this guide (and all his books). If you want him to get involved at your institution, he would would love to hear from you at steventhomasrook@yahho.co.uk.

Why experience matters

Contents

Useful links

On the web

The HE Careers Services Unit: www.hecsu.ac.uk – Look up 'The Impact of Work Experiences on HE Student Outcomes'

www.agr.org.uk – See the graduate recruitment news

On Twitter

Graduate Prospects: @Prospects

#graduateskills

Learning how to sing

Whether you're a singer, dancer, lawyer or judge, experience is the oil that keeps your career on track. It helps you identify interesting careers, develop your skills and promote what you have to offer.

What is experience?

Employment experience is any paid or unpaid activity which helps you develop your employment-related skills. When you're just starting out, you shouldn't be too proud to get your hands dirty with any reasonable, legal and ethical roles whatever they involve, wherever they're based and whatever the pay. Then, hopefully, as you build your CV and develop your skills you'll soon start earning a decent wage.

> 66 Experience is the oil that keeps your career on track. 99

What's in it for employers?

Experience is incredibly valuable to employers because it demonstrates your skills, commitment and knowledge and therefore your ability to succeed in the workplace i.e. your employability.

> **Laura Lodwick, Operations Manager,**
> **BJSS Limited**
>
> We look for candidates who have a good academic background but we are especially attracted to those who also have a wealth of experience – people who have gone out of their way to get wider experience and some general business awareness.

What's in it for you?

Experience can help you as follows:

Research a role

Get a real-life understanding of particular careers, roles and sectors. You won't get this from a thousand books and websites. Of course, you may not be able to get experience in the exact roles you want to enter, but any related experience will give you a deeper understanding of sectors and how they link to your goals and aspirations.

Develop your skills

Enhance the specific skills you'll need in your career, be it through study, hobbies, volunteering, work or internships. However, you will inevitably develop more relevant and marketable skills by gradually building up your employment portfolio to include experience which is closely linked to the role you want to enter.

Build contacts

Get to know key people such as fellow workers, teammates, supervisors, clients, customers, online contacts or just strangers in the corridors of power.

Undertake the experience required

Volunteering and working during your study may also be of use in building up the minimum experience that many employers demand. For example, if you spent your vacations for the last three years in the front office of a local theatre, you could legitimately argue that this constitutes the two years of experience required for a particular job in customer service.

Open doors

The fifth key benefit of experience is that, once you get your foot in the door of an organisation, you can talk your way into even better opportunities. For example:

- If you're liaising with a local charity in a voluntary role, you could ask them if they have any openings themselves.
- If you're working at a supermarket and a local estate agent walks in and asks where you keep the peas, you can ask her if she's got five minutes sometime for a chat about her job.

Steve Rook, author of this guide

I only fully appreciated the full value of experience when I was in my thirties (I'm a slow learner!). I'd done scores of jobs but they'd meant nothing more to me than a pay packet at the end of the week (we used to get paid in little brown envelopes).

At the time I was running my own business, recruiting teachers from Australia to work in the UK, and I came across the role of University Careers Advisers. I immediately thought the job was fantastic so I decided to give it a shot myself. Only, instead of just sending out a million applications (and getting a million rejections), I decided to develop a strategy involving experience and using my networks. This is how I got my foot in the door:

- I liaised even more closely with the careers advisers I already knew and volunteered to help them with their students.

- I discussed their roles.

- One of them offered to help me with applications and offer me a reference.

- I got a part-time job in the UK in a relatively uncompetitive role.

- I got the job and the rest is history!

Without the experience I organised, I wouldn't have got the help I needed and my applications would have been poor – they completely made the difference!

Why experience has grown in importance

A greater focus on skills

Since the early 1960s, the UK student body has expanded and diversified beyond all recognition.[1] Recruiters have adapted to this new paradigm by adjusting their recruitment processes in favour of an objective assessment of specific skills – as this is a fair and effective way to compare ability and potential. This, in turn, means that experience has also grown in importance because it is the most valuable barometer of what you can do.

How this affects you

Your role in the modern recruitment process is quite straightforward: Identify the skills you need in your chosen career (both technical and transferable), develop them through your experience and prove what you have to offer in each individual application.

The careers service at the University of Kent analysed various surveys to identify a straightforward top 10 of transferable 'employability' skills required by employers – these are listed below.[2] However, you should never forget that every role you go for will have unique requirements, which you should target (see Chapter 9).

Top 10 skills required by employers	
1. Verbal communication	6. Drive
2. Teamwork	7. Written communication
3. Commercial awareness	8. Planning and organisation
4. Analysing/Investigating	9. Flexibility
5. Initiative/Self-motivation	10. Time management

Your first steps

Now you have a better idea of the role of experience within recruitment, you have to get out there and get busy. It can be scary picking up the phone and asking for a job, approaching a university society or volunteering with a charity, but this is what you've got to do – and the sooner you get going, the better.

Once you've taken your first steps you'll soon realise there's nothing to it and you'll love the feeling of power that comes with taking control.

What to do now

Simple. Turn to the appropriate chapter and get going...

Good luck!

Chapter 1

Planning your route

Contents

Useful links

On the web

Target: www.targetjobs.co.uk – see 'Careers Advice'
Kent University Careers: www.kent.ac.uk/careers – see 'Career Planning'

On Twitter

#careerplanning
#careercoach
#career
#coaching
#careerchat

On YouTube

'How to Set Your Career Goals', by Project Management Videos
'Donald Trump's Advice on Choosing a Career', by bluveeta

Taking control

You get experience just by being alive. As a child you gradually get involved in ever-more sophisticated activities and meet a growing range of people, but once you start university, your world automatically expands. You see things, meet people and get involved in an ever-expanding world of sport, culture, relationships and work (not to mention study).

> 𝒢𝒢 You get experience just by being alive. 𝒥𝒥

This expanding experience is absolutely crucial in your journey towards employability, and three things give you a head start:

- All experience counts – everything you've ever done will help, from learning how to walk to a graduate internship.
- You've already started – even as you arrive on campus, you'll have millions of valuable experiences.
- There are numerous opportunities to get involved.

This chapter divides this pathway into four distinct steps. You can find out more about this process in *The Graduate Career Guidebook* (Rook, 2013).

Step 1: Identify your destination

The first part of any journey is figuring out where you want to go. In career terms, this means choosing the role and sector you want to target.

At first, this choice can be overwhelming because you're not just limited to roles directly related to your degree. In fact, 70 per cent of today's graduates go into roles totally unrelated to what they've studied at uni. Therefore, you have to search far and wide. However, if you just can't pinpoint the role you want to enter, don't panic. Try to at least narrow down your focus to a particular industry or sector, as this will really help you take control of your next steps. Use the following strategies:

Use your social networks

Ask friends and other contacts about the careers they've always found attractive and what they suggest for you. Also, look on hashtags such as #techjobs, #jobsinoxford and #guardianjobs.

Find your careers service

Pop into your university's careers service and ask for help, attend events or meet professionals in the field.

Brainstorm

Simply find a quiet place, sit down and see what comes to mind.

Take a look around

Just keep your eyes open for new ideas. You could also get involved in new activities or just watch TV and see what jobs come to mind, for example camera operators, actors and chefs.

Look up some graduate career websites

Look for interesting occupations on www.prospects.ac.uk and www. targetjobs.co.uk.

See what jobs you like

Look at the vacancies on offer at temp agencies, online job boards and graduate career websites to find any attractive roles. Links to these can be found in later chapters.

Assess yourself using online diagnostic tools

Identify suitable occupations using the interactive questionnaires at https://nationalcareersservice.direct.gov.uk and www.prospects.ac.uk/planner.

Identify degree-relevant roles

Your careers service can tell you what individual graduates in each degree discipline have done six months after graduation. You can also find degree-relevant occupations on Prospects.

Look at some postgraduate futures

Research postgrad courses to see what interesting careers they can herald.

Let the Internet search for you

See what comes up when you search terms such as 'alternative careers' or 'exciting jobs'.

'When I grow up ...'

Try to remember all your career dreams, even when you were a child and identify some similar roles that look interesting. For example, if you once dreamed of being a footballer, you could consider becoming a sports coach, reporter or psychologist.

Identify jobs linked to your interests

Think of opportunities linked to what you do in your spare time. For example, if you enjoy listening to friends' problems, why not consider counselling or social work?

Colonel David Thornycroft (retired)

Today's students and graduates need to have open minds about their opportunities in life and not feel confined to careers which are directly linked to what they studied at university. Employers look for more attributes than your specific academic knowledge; they are attracted to graduates because of their good all-round intelligence, the confidence to take control of events and the ability to analyse information and make logical deductions.

Step 2: See where you currently stand

Before heading straight for a chosen role or career, take a step back and systematically reflect on what you already have to offer (yes - you!) and how far down the road you already are. You'll almost certainly find that you already have far more of the experience, skills and qualifications required

To review your experience, try listing all the jobs, hobbies, travel and volunteering activities you've undertaken plus any projects you've been involved in at school and university. These could be everyday activities like helping your dad out at work, supporting a local charity, working a Saturday job at your local supermarket, participating in the school enterprise society or playing cricket for your local team. These straightforward experiences don't sound like much, but they are all valuable milestones on your journey into a career, and you should give them due respect, so list them below. You can complete the exercise right here or download it from the companion website at www.palgravecareerskills.com.

Self-assessment: What have you done so far to further your career?

List 10 activities you've already undertaken that will help you in your career (think of everything from jobs and volunteering to sport, pastimes, travel and clubs). Make sure you fill up the table.

Your existing experience:	
1.	6.
2.	7.
3.	8.
4.	9.
5.	10.

Reflecting on your answers: Students often think they've done very little so far to advance their careers when they actually have a wealth of useful experiences. So, if you're struggling to come up with examples - have a chat with a careers adviser.

As far as your qualifications are concerned, think of what you've done at school and uni that will help you in your chosen role.

To reflect on your skills, mull over your experiences and qualifications, and systematically identify the skills they've imparted. Remember, skills aren't just long words to put on your CV, such as 'communication' and 'negotiation'; neither are they simply what you've done. They are your unique, practical abilities that enable you to thrive in every walk of life. By definition (as you're alive), you have millions of them.

Now, link your recent experiences to your personal attributes in the table below. For example, playing rugby for the university may have really given you commitment and the ability to work in a team, whereas an innovation award at work may have made you more enterprising and able to solve problems. You can complete the exercise right here or download it from the companion website at www.palgravecareerskills.com.

Self-assessment: What you have to offer

Outline the skills you've gained from two recent experiences.

Your experience	Three skills you gained and demonstrated (avoid jargon such as 'teamwork', 'leadership'...)
	1. 2. 3.
	1. 2. 3.

Reflecting on your answers: If you had trouble teasing out your own abilities, ask your family and friends for help, as you have to get used to appraising your own strengths in this objective way.

Step 3: Plan how to get from A to B

Once you have a good understanding of where you want to go in your career and what you have to offer, you can develop a personalised plan of action.

To evaluate the experience, qualifications and skills you'll need in your chosen career, check out the various routes people take. You can do this using the following tools:

- www.prospects.ac.uk (Look under 'Types of jobs' in the section on 'Jobs and work experience')
- www.nationalcareersservice.direct.gov.uk – see 'Job profiles'
- Websites of relevant professional organisations
- Contacts who know about particular sectors and roles
- Employers at careers events
- Your careers service.

When you do start looking into things, you'll soon see that there are now numerous paths into most professional roles. These could involve a vast array of courses, work experience, internships and professional training. For example, to become a lawyer you could sign up for a series of postgraduate courses and look for a training contract, become a legal executive and then transfer or start out as a paralegal. Therefore, don't just automatically plump for the most travelled path; because you're an individual with unique attributes and aspirations and alternative routes may be far more suitable (see Sigourney's story opposite).

At the start of your journey, you may plan to get involved in activities such as volunteering, university societies, part-time work and holiday jobs. Then, as you build up your CV, you may want to develop your roles further and look for positions of responsibility, find internships, sign up for a postgraduate course and/or work overseas. The world is your oyster! Each of these activities is outlined in detail in the chapters that follow.

Self-assessment: Identifying skills you need to develop

Research the career you want to pursue, and list five specific technical and transferable skills you still need to develop.

The sector/role: _____

Technical skills required	Transferable skills required
1.	1.
2.	2.
3.	3.
4.	4.
5.	5.

In terms of the skills you'll need to enhance, some will be technically related to the particular role, and others will be transferable between industries. For example, quantity surveyors will need to understand specific equipment and be able to work in teams. Use the resources provided to identify the key skills you'll need. You can complete the exercise right here or download it from the companion website at www.palgravecareerskills.com.

Chapter 2

Sigourney Chippendale – trainee teacher

At the end of university I made a last-minute decision to go travelling abroad and visit Australia. As I travelled alone, this helped me grow as a person and build on my character and independence. This, in turn, helped me take control of my career. I had a growing interest in becoming a teacher, but I wanted to make sure this was the right career path for me. Therefore, for a whole year I worked as a teaching assistant, just to make sure. I am now on a school-based teacher training course and greatly enjoy being a role model, making school a positive experience for children.

Step 4: Get started

You can take up numerous roles to develop your skills. Start by assessing your current attributes, what's on offer, how experiences will look on your CV and your chances of being accepted.

Unfortunately, the best opportunities, such as internships at major organisations, are often very competitive. Therefore, if you're struggling to get your foot in the door, don't just keep on applying for the same roles; take a few steps back and look for more basic opportunities. You'll soon make rapid progress.

For example, if you want to be a journalist, you may think the first step is an internship at a national newspaper, but in all probability, you'd first have to write numerous articles for print and online media for which you'll need experience, such as a voluntary role on your university paper and so on...

Now it's your turn

Look over the example career plan provided overleaf, and design your own career journey over the following pages. On your personal career itinerary, include as many details as possible about the courses and professional training, experience and networking opportunities you plan to undertake plus the skills you hope to develop. You can complete the exercise right here or download it from the companion website at www.palgravecareerskills.com.

Of course, once you've embarked on your career path, you'll probably change direction as you go, but don't worry: it can still really help to have a plan in mind before you head off. Again, if you're still not sure what career you want to go into, just focus on a sector or industry that looks attractive.

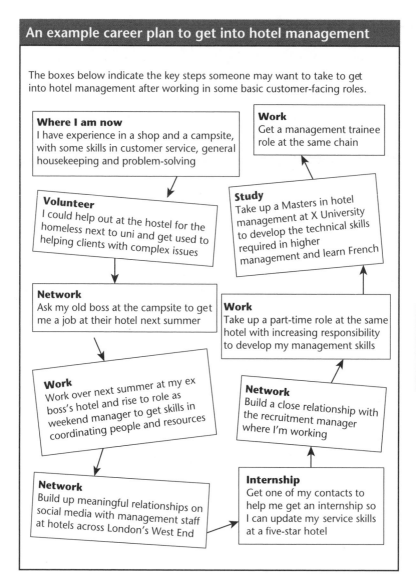

An example career plan to get into hotel management

The boxes below indicate the key steps someone may want to take to get into hotel management after working in some basic customer-facing roles.

Where I am now
I have experience in a shop and a campsite, with some skills in customer service, general housekeeping and problem-solving

Work
Get a management trainee role at the same chain

Volunteer
I could help out at the hostel for the homeless next to uni and get used to helping clients with complex issues

Study
Take up a Masters in hotel management at X University to develop the technical skills required in higher management and learn French

Network
Ask my old boss at the campsite to get me a job at their hotel next summer

Work
Take up a part-time role at the same hotel with increasing responsibility to develop my management skills

Work
Work over next summer at my ex boss's hotel and rise to role as weekend manager to get skills in coordinating people and resources

Network
Build a close relationship with the recruitment manager where I'm working

Network
Build up meaningful relationships on social media with management staff at hotels across London's West End

Internship
Get one of my contacts to help me get an internship so I can update my service skills at a five-star hotel

Chapter 2

Self-assessment: Plan out your career path

Map out some possible steps into your chosen career. Be as specific as possible about what's involved and what you plan to gain (i.e. the skills, qualifications and opportunities) plus set a date. Include:

- Four experiences such as clubs and societies, work experience, volunteering, internships and further study.
- Two networking activities including whom you plan to contact and the help you hope they'll provide.

Be as specific as possible.

Your destination (the career role you're seeking)
....
Due date:

Step 1:
What's involved: ....
....
What you'll gain: ....
....
Due date:

Step 6:
What's involved: ....
....
....
What you'll gain: ....
....
....
Due date:

Step 5:
What's involved: ....
....
....
What you'll gain: ....
....
....
Due date:

Chapter 2

Step 2:
What's involved: ....
....
What you'll gain: ....
....

Due date:

Step 3:
What's involved: ....
....
What you'll gain: ....
....

Due date:

Step 4:
What's involved: ....
....
What you'll gain: ....
....

Due date:

Chapter 2

Chapter 2

Paul Harper, Graduate Advantage, www.graduateadvantage.co.uk

Employers desire professional, work-ready graduates who understand business etiquette and possess commercial awareness, relevant skills and experience. Many UK universities, such as Aston, have responded to this, offering increased support to students. However, your university can only provide a proportion of what you need ... you need to consider your own employability journey!

This should begin in your first year of study, considering the activities available, the relevant skills or experience you may develop and managing activities effectively alongside your studies.

Activities could include volunteering in the local community, society membership, becoming a student ambassador, part-time employment, summer employment/internships, mentoring schemes and careers service appointments and activities.

When considering study commitments, your employability journey plan may resemble something similar to this:

Year 1 – volunteering, society membership, summer/part-time work
Year 2 – mentoring, plus summer/part-time work
Year 3 – placement in industry (if available)
Year 4 – careers appointments, planning and making applications

With all planning complete, throughout your journey you will need to reflect on what you have done so far, new skills or experience gained and notable achievements. It is vital that you record these on your CV. These will build throughout your journey making you increasingly attractive to that prospective future employer. As with many journeys you may find you divert off course at times. Simply re-evaluate what is needed to get you back on track and you will eventually reach your chosen destination. Plan, Participate, Reflect and Re-evaluate – the key to a successful employability journey. Make every experience count!

What to do now

Get going! Sometimes, the more time you spend planning a journey, the more insurmountable it can seem. So, once you've developed a rough career plan, throw your car into gear and head off down the highway.

Managing your networks and social media

Contents

Useful links

On the web

See '10 social media habits' on: www.blog.suny.edu

See '20 Social media marketing tips' on www.socialmediaexaminer.com

On Twitter

@careersbham

@LeedsUniCareers

The times they are a-changing

It's always been important to know the right people, especially when it comes to finding fulfilling employment. Therefore, well-connected students and graduates have always had the edge.

However, if your dad isn't the head of Boots and your mum's not Madonna, you still have hope. Society has diversified over recent years to allow greater interaction between people, and the Internet has heralded a host of effective new communication channels. Therefore, there's unprecedented scope to meet the people who matter. So, get chatting and fill up your address book. You just need to reach out and get in touch.

> 💬 You just need to reach out and get in touch. 💬

What are networks?

Networks are 'groups of people who exchange contacts and experience for professional or social purposes'.[1] The word comes from the arrangement of horizontal and vertical lines on a fishing net and therefore implies that we are all connected through an ever-widening latticework of links. This was brilliantly demonstrated by the Hungarian playwright Frigyes Karinthy in 1929, when he showed that even with the flimsiest of networks, every person on the planet is just six links away from everyone else.[2]

Why networks are important

Employers are investing heavily in their networks in order to effectively advertise vacancies, keep in touch with applicants and find effective staff. They're actively beefing up their online networks and finding new ways to meet students and graduates in person. This is because they realise the benefits of finding the very best applicants in a competitive market. This, in turn, enables students and graduates from every sector of society to raise their profiles and get noticed. The collective value of your networks and the benefits they deliver is called your *social capital*.

Who you should know

There are certain contacts that almost everybody should have in their networks:

- Friends
- Family
- Colleagues and managers
- Lecturers and careers advisers
- Professionals in your chosen sector or any field
- Recruiters
- Representatives of professional organisations (such as The Chartered Institute of Marketing)
- Other students and graduates.

However, you also need to tailor your network to your unique character, situation and aspirations. For example:

- If your mum works in the field you want to enter, then you should definitely get in touch with her friends and colleagues.
- If you want to work overseas, you should probably look out for interesting businesses and expat communities in the region.

The following pages outline how you can effectively manage your networks in each area of your life, in other words:

- Your personal interactions
- Your online networks in general
- Facebook®, Twitter® and LinkedIn®
- Blogs and other social media channels.

Each of these networks is explored in terms of:

- Why they're important
- How you can develop your brand
- Building and using your network.

The key issues are then tied together to help you develop a joined-up networking strategy.

Your personal interactions

Why they're important

Nowadays, when most students and graduates think of networking, they immediately turn to apps such as Twitter, LinkedIn and Facebook. However, you shouldn't underestimate the value of older technologies such as phones, texts and paper and ink. Also, never forget the powerful influence you can wield just by meeting people in person. This is still the best way to build up real and meaningful relationships that will help you get the experience you need.

Developing your brand

Recruiters will judge your book by its cover. Therefore, if you seem lazy, careless and ignorant, that's how you'll be treated. So, before reaching out to employers, take some time to honestly appraise the image you're currently portraying to others, and up your game. You may also want to ask others what they think. You don't have to totally abandon your character; you just need to interact positively, try to be charming and present your best features. Above all, you should be:

- Well-spoken
- Attentive
- Friendly, positive, respectful and professional
- Polite, but not so formal that you seem subservient or uncomfortable
- Well dressed in appropriate garb (of good quality)

- Clean
- Well-shaven (if you need to be).

Jonathan May, student

When I started university, I felt so awkward talking to people. I come from a little village, and I've known most people there my whole life, so meeting employers and business people was quite daunting. I didn't know what to say, what to wear or how to act, so I just avoided any interactions. However, once I met a few friendly employers on my course and at work, I started to feel more comfortable and started to chat to professional people whenever I got the chance. Now, I don't feel so uncomfortable in my suit and can chat more naturally, so looking for a job isn't nearly as stressful.

If you're socially awkward when meeting employers, you can feel better if you:

- Focus on the areas of social interaction where you feel most comfortable.
- Practise in safe settings (such as a university society).
- Ask careers advisers for help.
- Slowly and gradually embed yourself in the industry you want to enter.

Building your network

The people you know and the people they know Start building your network by identifying any immediate acquaintances who may be able to help. Such personal contacts are especially valuable because they have a real motivation to lend you a hand. However, don't worry if you can't think of anyone in the exact sector you want to enter, as not many students do. Contacts from any field will be able to help by:

- Giving you experience albeit in an unrelated area where you'll still learn the skills you require.
- Putting you in touch with people who are in the sector you want to enter.
- Putting you in touch with people who know other people who are involved in the sector you want to enter.

For example, your old boss may be able to give you a temporary job; your aunt's best friend may know someone who needs a volunteer; or your boss's accountant's wife could be looking for an intern. Either way, you don't know until you ask.

Try coming up with some possible new career contacts in the following exercise. If you take your time and think creatively, you are almost guaranteed to come up with some excellent leads. You can complete the exercise right here or download it from the companion website at www.palgravecareerskills.com.

Self-assessment: Possible new contacts

In the tables below, identify three possible new contacts who may have some sort of connection to your chosen career.

1. Someone you know directly who may be able to help

2. Someone you know who may know someone who could help	
Someone you know	Someone they may know (either a specific person or someone in a particular role, such as 'doctor')

3. Someone you know who may know someone who may know someone else who could help		
Someone you know	Someone they may know (specific person or role)	Someone they may know (specific (person or role)

Reflecting on your answers: If you're stuck, put yourself in your contacts' shoes and imagine who they interact with on a daily basis – plus get some friends to help.

> ### Alison Richardson,
> ### Senior People Services Adviser, NNL
>
> The standard of applications is steadily rising therefore you need to find more ways to stand out from the crowd and sell yourself effectively. A very good way to do this is to communicate confidently and engagingly. For example, if you approach representatives of organisations at fairs show you have done your research, ask them perceptive questions and generally demonstrate an ability to build rapport.

Casting your net wider Once you've exhausted your immediate circle of acquaintances, it's time to look further afield.

For example, if you want to become a manager for a group of musicians, you could help organise band nights at uni, chat to people behind the scenes at gigs and start up a band yourself. Find out more on page 64.

> ### Darren Childs, recent graduate
>
> The biggest employer where I live is British Aerospace, so it's not surprising I always wanted to work there. However, when they came to a careers event, their stall was three deep all day! I just couldn't chat. However, I saw an advert in my local paper about an open day for the public at their local workshop. I couldn't believe my luck. When I turned up, I was almost the only person there, and I chatted to at least 20 workers and managers, getting some great contacts and advice.

Overcoming hurdles Unfortunately, many jobseekers still have an inbuilt disadvantage when it comes to mixing with employers in their chosen profession. For example:

- Applicants from poorer, non-professional families may lack social capital because they simply aren't accustomed to mixing in the right circles and don't know how to behave.

- Older jobseekers and those from an under-represented gender or ethnic background may face prejudice.
- People who haven't embraced social media may not have the facility to join the conversation.

If you feel left out of society for whatever reason, you owe it to yourself to fight the powers that be. This involves being persistent and purposefully developing your brand and social capital so you 'fit in'. Just walking around in ill-fitting suits and shouting, 'What's up?' to graduate recruiters will get you absolutely nowhere. Ask for help from anyone who can understand and appreciate your particular difficulties, such as:

- People in your family
- Your university careers service (which may have specific mentoring groups for people in your situation)
- Specific student societies (such as The Jewish Society)
- Local or national mentoring groups for people from your community, such as The Aspire Foundation, for women, at www. aspirewomen.co.uk.

Using your network

Becoming more visible Employers don't tend to pop round to people's houses offering employment (and you should be suspicious if they do). You need to get out there and mingle. Mix with friends, friends of friends, colleagues, managers, lecturers and any professional contacts you've managed to generate.

Building closer ties When you're socialising with friends and meeting new contacts, don't just live in the present and have a good time. Proactively look for opportunities to provide assistance for people so they'll be inclined to help you when the time comes. You needn't view this as being overly manipulative or insincere. People have been scratching each other's backs for centuries. You can build closer ties by staying in touch when you meet new people, joining in with their activities, inviting them to events and just helping out in any way you can.

Asking for help Once you've built up a relationship with your contacts, it's time to ask for some help in return. However, take things slowly, as you don't want to scare them off. For example, you could

Chapter 3

ask for a chat about a particular career, whether they know anywhere you could get some experience or voluntary work and if they could put you in touch with other people who could lend a hand. Then, further down the line, you could ask for more significant experience and/or an internship.

Five-minute chats One effective networking strategy is to arrange short meetings with people to discuss their roles. These get-togethers are often formally called 'informational interviews'. Just get in touch with relevant contacts (by telephone or in person if possible), tell them your mum is one of their clients (if she is), and ask if you can pop in to see them for five minutes to discuss their careers. Then, when you meet them, you can ask what's involved in their roles, the skills you need to develop, how to get your foot in the door and so on. Finally, you can ask for more help, such as an opportunity to shadow them at work. You'll be surprised how successful this strategy can be, especially if you've already laid the groundwork by building closer ties.

Shadowing As the title suggests, this involves observing a contact at work for a day or two and seeing what this person gets up to. It's a

great way to get a real sense of what a particular job is like. Of course, it's also a wonderful opportunity to impress people in the organisation, show you're interested and meet more useful contacts. You can tee up this sort of opportunity through your existing contacts or when you meet new people. Then, before you leave, you could offer to perform some sort of role for them in your time off, for example a more structured experience and/or an internship.

To find out more about personal networking, see 'The dos and don'ts of student networking' at www.guardian.co.uk and 'Developing networking skills' at www.brunel.ac.uk.

Your social networks (in general)

Why they're important

Over an incredibly short period of time, social media have quickly become absolutely crucial weapons in your networking arsenal.

Employers use social networks to promote their opportunities and identify talent. For example, Jobvite[3] recently found that 93 per cent of recruiters take candidates' social profiles into account in their hiring decisions and 55 per cent of employers changed their decisions based on what they've found.

These new social networks have given students and graduates unparalleled opportunities to raise their profiles, get experience and find careers. Therefore, it's a win–win situation, unless, of course, like 60 per cent of the workforce,[4] you don't have an effective social media strategy. So, read on to make sure you're pulling all the right strings.

Developing your brand

Your social media brand is just as important as your real-life image, perhaps even more so because there's no room for subtlety and nuance. Decisions about you will be made in nanoseconds, so you better look the part. Some key principles to follow across your social platform profiles are as follows:

Use a professional and consistent image Upload the same picture of yourself onto each of your platforms so people quickly start to recognise you and get used to seeing you around. Use a friendly photo, and present yourself in the same way as popular professionals in the field you want to enter. Avoid any shade or glare and sunglasses, but squint your eyes slightly. You can assess the effectiveness of your images on www.photofeeler.com. You can also enhance your search engine optimisation by naming your photo file appropriately, for example 'SteveRook.jpg'.

Keep the same name and username Use your real name on all your profiles because this looks professional, you'll be easily found and names are used to rank profiles on search engines. Consider using a nickname if you have a common name and you fear being lost in the throng. However, make sure you're consistent, and highlight your real name somewhere on each profile. Also, try to find a consistent, short, memorable and descriptive username which represents what you have to offer (professionally). You can check whether names are universally available on several websites and apps such as www.knowem.com.

Develop an impressive and noticeable profile A presence on social media can actually be counterproductive if it doesn't show you off in a good light. Therefore, if you're going to paste your brand all over the Internet, do it right. First of all, use any written sections to sell yourself, especially your bio/headline/summary. This is your 'elevator' pitch to recruiters, so it's crucial you use keywords which will be picked up. Focus on words and phrases for the following:

- Your name and job title
- Previous job titles
- Your target employers
- Previous employers
- Your location/target location
- Your qualifications
- Your skills
- Industry jargon and news.

Some possible keywords

- Jane Simpson
- Media analyst
- IT project manager
- London
- Diploma in social work
- DipSW

- PwC
- Accounting technician
- BSc chemistry
- Teamwork
- Sales

One good way to find good keywords in your sector is to look for commonly used words and phrases in relevant job adverts. Try to be as specific as possible and avoid vague clichés such as 'experienced marketing professional' or 'dynamic salesperson'. Come up with some possible keywords for your social profiles in the following exercise. You can complete the exercise right here or download it from the companion website at www.palgravecareerskills.com.

Self-assessment: Social media keywords

List 10 effective keywords for your social network profiles that will be noticed by recruiters.

Your keywords	
1.	6.
2.	7.
3.	8.
4.	9.
5.	10.

Reflecting on your answers: Assess your answers by searching on the Internet for various combinations of the words you've identified and seeing how many job adverts you unearth.

Don't just fill out the main sections on each of your profiles – be thorough as this, again, will optimise your pages in any employer searches and demonstrate a good all-round impression. Additional media elements such as pictures, videos and presentations will also boost your image (as long as they're on message and support your brand).

Do the shake and vac, and put the freshness back Make sure everything on your networks is clean and decent. Obviously, you should delete any pictures that don't put you in a positive light and any swear words, but also remove any rants and articles and posts that are

- contentious,
- offensive and/or rude, or
- off the wall.

Again, there are a number of online tools to help you clean up your act, such as www.simplewa.sh.

Customise your background On some channel profiles, such as Twitter and YouTube®, you can upload customised backgrounds. This allows you to portray your brand even more effectively. For example, if you're an engineer, you could upload a scene where you're working on a particularly impressive project. Also, you could design a picture with extra links and icons to your other networks.

Control your settings and permissions You have to take an active decision over who'll be able to see your information and interactions. Don't just 'publish and be damned'. Obviously, the wider you distribute your messages, the more effectively you can network. To give your channels any hope of success, you should, at least, release your bio, summary and profile picture. If you feel the need to share lots of dodgy content, you may want to set up two profiles on each channel (private and public) just to avoid any cross-contamination.

Building your network

Don't just rush in like Tonto and get as many contacts as you can; they'll probably be of little assistance, and you'll dilute your brand. Take your time to put together a targeted, effective group of contacts which you can manage effectively. You can use specific strategies on each platform to widen your circle of contacts (as outlined in the following pages). However, the general principles are the same for all media as they are in real life:

- Join up with your existing contacts either manually or by extracting them from your various email providers.
- Sign up to relevant groups, join conversations and connect with any interesting people you encounter.
- Publish interesting information and news relevant to the career you're seeking, which will draw people to you.
- Link your real-life interactions and various social networking channels so you can draw together people from all areas of your life (see 'A joined-up networking strategy', later in this chapter).
- Get busy: Proactively look for opportunities to join up with interesting people.

Using your network

Get started Just as with your personal interactions, you should gradually build up rapport with contacts before asking for help. This takes time, but the tortoise always wins, so get busy. You can build up your relationships on all social media as follows:

- Join conversations.
- Build up a following, and identify more substantial links.
- Help people out, and gradually build up mutually beneficial relationships.
- Ask for advice and guidance.

Whatever you do, don't just spam everyone in your first week online, asking for a job.

Interact Don't just set up your accounts and never look at them again. Get in touch with people on a regular basis. Come up with interesting tidbits to share, and respond immediately to other people's posts and queries. In other words, don't just add friends and join groups – participate. However, remember to keep everything light-hearted, fun and clean.

At first, it'll be easy to manage your networks on an ad hoc basis by typing in a few messages every now and again and responding when your phone goes ping. However, pretty soon you're going to have to get on top of things. You can manage your networks in several ways:

Focus A well-managed presence on a few key accounts is far more effective than weak profiles on every platform out there. As far as career planning is concerned, you should at least be a major player on Twitter and LinkedIn.

Coordinate and schedule There are several social media management systems which you can use to bring all your social networking accounts together in one place so you can quickly keep track of what's going on and schedule messages. You may want to look at https://buffer.com and https://hootsuite.com.

Promote your networks Add links to your profiles in your business cards, CVs and all other online activities including your email signature.

Establish a holding page Choose one central place for a detailed account of what you can offer. This could be your own website or your LinkedIn profile.

To find out more about networking on social media, see 'How social media can boost your professional profile' at www.theguardian.com and 'Social and digital networking' at www.brad.ac.uk.

Facebook

Why it's important

Facebook is the biggest social networking tool, with over 1.25 billion users across the world.[5] However, it's primarily used as a social networking channel rather than a professional network. It's a place to keep in touch with friends and share experiences and opinions. Nonetheless, it can be especially helpful at the start of your experience journey to raise your profile and help you get involved in all sorts of activities.

Developing your brand

When you sign up for Facebook, take a few minutes to enter a professional email address where employers can find you, and a link to your 'holding page', where you keep up-to-date information about your experience, skills, qualifications and so on. This will probably be your LinkedIn profile or website.

Once you've filled out all the basic information on your status, you can jump straight into contacting your friends. However, right from the start, you should take steps to stay on top of how you're perceived. This is because even if employers don't recruit through the channel, they will almost certainly use it to look into prospective employees, and if you're tagged in a hundred semi-clad pictures, chugging bottles of vodka, your chances may be limited. There are three things you can do to keep your brand positive and clean:

- Set appropriate privacy settings, and regularly review your 'Activity log'. In particular, limit your posts to friends, and delete unbecoming photographs that have been tagged.
- Post regularly, presenting yourself as an outgoing, friendly person with varied interests and appropriate values.
- Post about topics related to your chosen career.
- Report back from career-relevant events and activities.
- Avoid drunk posting!

Building your network

It's relatively straightforward to meet people on Facebook. You can start just by interacting with the people you already know and joining up with anyone else whose comments and contributions you enjoy. You can also look at friends' connections and see if they want to join up with you, as well as join groups linked to your school, university, interests and interesting career paths. In the following exercise, identify some really exciting contacts related to your interests and aspirations. You can complete the exercise right here or download it from the companion website at www.palgravecareerskills.com.

Self-assessment: Possible new Facebook friends

1 Do an Internet search on your favourite interests and industries to identify four dream Facebook contacts (try to find specific people who genuinely get you excited).
2 Figure out how you might be able to get in touch, for example through particular groups, and consider other possible contacts who are well connected (take your time to find specific links).

Who you'd love to contact	How you could possibly get in touch
1.	
2.	
3.	
4.	

Chapter 3

Using your network

You can join up with people and organisations on Facebook to accomplish the following:

- Research employer expectations.
- Widen your circle of friends to the sectors you want to enter.
- Initiate professional relationships.
- Get involved in activities such as employer events on campus.
- Get involved in volunteering events.
- Communicate with people to find opportunities.
- Chat on an informal basis to professionals.

Twitter

Why it's important

Twitter is less than 10 years old and has quickly become one of the best tools for students and graduates at every stage in their career journeys, whether they're just starting out or looking for blue-ribbon internships. This is because it's a great tool to research careers, get noticed and find a job.

Its success is down to its democratic, non-hierarchical structure and the strict limit on the length of messages (140 characters). This gives you quick and easy access to people and organisations in any area of industry and recruitment, including these:

- Professionals
- Professional organisations
- Recruiters
- Students and graduates
- Trainees
- Careers advisers
- News organisations

The great benefit of Twitter for people just starting out is that you can get a real feel for different careers in an easy-going environment, meet people who are at your stage in the journey and contact organisations who want to hear from you. The sooner you start, the deeper you can embed yourself for when you need an internship or more formal experience, so get going!

It can take a bit of time getting used to the jargon on Twitter, but don't let this put you off. Some of the key terms are outlined in the following table.

A Glossary of Twitter terms	
Tweet	These are your messages – you're allowed up to 140 characters of text plus photos, videos and links.
Username/ Twitter handle	This is what you call yourself – it's always preceded by the @ symbol, e.g. '@stevenrook'.
#	This symbol is attached to the beginning of a word, which turns the word into a hashtag (see below).
Hashtag	Words or amalgamations of words which are preceded by a '#' symbol, such as '#jobs' and '#CareerPlanning'. Hashtags are very useful because they generate a theme of tweets which you can search through (via the search tool) to research issues and promote what you have to say (where you'll be seen). Anyone can allocate hashtags, including you.
Followers	The people and organisations who have subscribed to other users' accounts so they can see their tweets. Any registered user can normally 'follow' any other (unless you've been blocked). Just click the 'Follow' button next to a user's name or on their profile page.
RT (retweet)	These are tweets you forward to your followers. There are various ways to retweet, where you can either just forward the message or add your own comments. The retweet button has two circling arrows and looks like a recycling symbol.
DM (direct messages)	These are private messages between users or groups.
Favouriting	By indicating you like tweets, you let the users who have shared them know you've approved; favouriting also stores them together so you can access them at any time.

A fuller appendix of terms and guidelines can be found on the Twitter website at www.twitter.com.

Developing your brand

Focus on how you can engage effectively with recruiters and employers. A scattering of banter on wider topics is okay because it shows you have a personality, but if you want to chat at length about your other interests, do so on another account.

The four most important aspects of your profile are your photo, account name, username and bio. Photos are covered in the previous section; advice on each of the other elements is provided next.

Your account name and username Twitter gives you two names which appear next to all your tweets.

Your account name can be 20 characters long and doesn't have to be unique, so you can just choose your real name, even if it's very common, for example 'John Smith' or 'Jane Doe'.

Usernames, on the other hand, can only be 15 characters long, have to be unique and are preceded by an '@'. So, again, you can simply choose your name, for example '@jsmith' or '@JaneDoe'. However, if your name is already taken (as these examples probably are), you could amend it or promote something like a blog, society or business, for example you could call yourself @Joeysoap or @TaxAccountant.

Two factors that should affect your choice of names:

- You should be consistent across all your social media accounts.
- When you retweet other peoples' tweets, only your username is included.

Your bio Twitter gives you just 160 characters to introduce yourself, what you have to offer and the job you're seeking, so think carefully about how you can use keywords to attract your target audience (i.e. recruiters). General keyword advice is provided in the previous section, but in terms of Twitter, you may want to include the following:

- Your university (especially if it's well regarded in your subject/the career you want to enter).
- Whom you work for and what you do (especially if you're an intern).

- Any awards you've gained.
- Your relevant interests.
- A link to your LinkedIn page (if you don't have a website), so people can find out more.

For example, your bio could look like this:

> ## Georgina Flowinski
> **@GFlow Portsmouth, UK**
>
> *Bournemouth Uni web interface designer. Volunteer at Shelter & RSPCA seeks internship with high-transaction platforms & mobile/ wearable technologies*
>
> uk.linkedin.com/in/GFlow

You can review more bios just by searching on images for 'good student Twitter bio'.

Building your network

Gradually get involved in the key discussions in your sector, as follows:

- Join up with your existing contacts.
- Get used to all the terms, buttons and procedures.
- Find organisations and individuals who actively publish interesting and useful tweets. These could be students, recruiters, careers services, businesses, professional groups or a wide range of other entities.
- Find other interesting individuals, organisations and hashtags to follow. You can do this in two main ways:
  - Identify who's being regularly retweeted by your existing contacts.
  - See whom your existing contacts are already following.
- Identify a manageable range of organisations and hashtags, and follow them regularly.
- Respond to tweets by offering help and advice and get used to incorporating the appropriate hashtags.

- Start sending your own tweets, but make sure they're always positive, interesting, relevant and newsworthy. A little humour also goes a long way.
- Retweet interesting posts, especially those by influential people. Some good advice from the BBC on this is to use an executive's Twitter handle to alert him or her to an article by adding potentially interested parties at the end of the tweet.[6]
- Remember to use your keywords so you can easily be found.
- Maintain a steady level of engagement so you become a familiar presence.

Research some useful Twitter links for your chosen industry in the following exercise. You can complete the exercise right here or download it from the companion website at www.palgravecareerskills.com.

Self-assessment: Interesting Twitter usernames and hashtags

1 In the table below, research your target career and identify:
   - Four interesting Twitter users (individuals and/or organisations) who publish useful tweets and retweets
   - Four useful hashtags

Users with interesting Twitter threads	Useful hashtags
1. @..	#...
2. @..	#...
3. @..	#...
4. @..	#...

Reflecting on your answers: Ask yourself how these links can help you develop your networking and job search strategy.

Using your network

Hopefully your urbane, helpful and interesting conversations on Twitter will attract employers like bees to honey, but you may also want to chivvy them along a bit. Once you've built up a bit of reputation, start asking around whether people know where you could get some experience, and contact key people to ask for a chat.

To find out more about networking on Twitter, see 'Using Twitter' on www.ed.ac.uk and 'How to find a graduate job using Twitter' on www.targetjobs.co.uk.

LinkedIn

Why it's important

LinkedIn has over 300 million members,[7] and in the UK, it's used by almost all of the big firms in their search for new talent (and most of the small ones too). Therefore, it's also a valuable tool for students and graduates to network and research occupations, industries and career paths. Your LinkedIn page is also a brilliant place to outline everything you have to offer in detail and can therefore also be seen as a virtual CV, especially if you use it as your 'landing' page, that is you link to it from all your other social networking sites.

LinkedIn is especially helpful once you're in the hunt for internships and graduate roles for these reasons:

- Employers directly advertise their posts.
- Organisations and recruiters discuss their roles and requirements.
- You can proactively seek out opportunities.
- Companies are increasingly getting out there and approaching people on spec even those who are not even looking for work (this is called 'passive' recruitment).

Developing your brand

Your profile on LinkedIn is much more substantial than most other platforms, and you should take time to sell yourself thoroughly by saturating every section with more keywords than The Concise Oxford English Dictionary.

> 𝘎𝘎 Saturate every section with more keywords than The Concise Oxford English Dictionary. 𝟿𝟿

LinkedIn gives you feedback on your 'profile strength' in a circle at the top right-hand corner of your page, based upon how much of it you've completed. You need to attain the highest status, that is 'all star'. This is more important than it sounds because when employers search for talent with certain keywords such as 'London', 'accountant', 'student' and 'intern', they'll get thousands of hits, but the profiles that have an 'all-star' status will be on page 1 – and who looks past that?

So, get busy and fill in every section. Advice is provided here on how to fill out the key sections, but start looking for ideas on the profiles of other student and graduates in your situation.

In general Your LinkedIn profile should be slightly less formal than your CV, so it's more sociable and personal. For example, you could use the first person and write as you would speak in person. Also, upload images, video or other elements that represent what you're about, especially if you're trying to get into the creative industries. This adds a bit of colour.

Your address Make sure you customise your public profile URL to your name when you set up your page.

The photo See the section above on your social networks in general.

The headline This is the short section (140 characters), just under your name, where you can attract employers' attention. As it's at the top of your profile, it's the first thing recruiters tend to look at, and you'll have a nanosecond to draw them in or lose them forever – so it has to be attractive. LinkedIn automatically lists your job title and employer, but you can override the default text so you sell yourself effectively to the specific employers you're trying to target. Also, make it clear you're looking for a job (unless you don't want your current employer to know). For example, you could write something like this:

> 𝘎𝘎 Student at Warwick University I Digital marketing specialist I Seeks internship I Experience of social media, PPC, SEO, video, content, PR and advertising. 𝟿𝟿

The summary Here, LinkedIn advises you to: 'Describe what motivates you, what you're skilled at, and what's next.' It's your opportunity to expand on your brand by outlining your accomplishments, strengths, ambitions and interests, and tying them to the industry you're looking to enter. A good example summary is shown below of a student at Boston College (without all the registered trademark signs).[8]

> 66 A second-year marketing undergraduate student at Boston College with an interest in marketing, advertising, and social media. Seeking a summer internship to apply my experience, assisting a company's branding needs through social media outreach, developing marketing plans, digital marketing and conducting customer research.
>
> Specialties:
> ● Event planning
> ● Social networking and marketing
> ● Account management
> ● Microsoft Office® (Word®, PowerPoint®, Excel®)
> ● Adobe CS5.5 Suite® (Photoshop®, Flash®) 99

Experience, organisations, education, interests . . . Complete *all* the remaining sections, including those designed for students, such as 'Courses', 'Projects', 'Languages' and 'Certificates'.

Write your profile as if it's a very short CV. Don't just list everything you've ever done, but focus on your experiences and achievements that put you in a positive light with employers in your chosen industry, and outline the relevant technical and transferable skills. For example:

● Focus on your pertinent tasks in previous jobs.
● List your relevant modules, research and dissertations.

LinkedIn has a facility to upload your CV in your experience section, but be careful. Make sure you adjust the resulting text so it promotes you effectively.

Recommendations Get employers, academics and influential contacts to put in a good word for you.

Skills Identify and list about 20 skills that are relevant to your industry so people can endorse you – and make sure you return the favour when they do.

Building your network

LinkedIn is a close-knit network of professional contacts. Therefore, when you join up, don't just reach out to anyone and everyone. Stick to people you already know, close contacts and people who will be happy to get in touch, such as alumni from your school or university and HR or recruitment professionals.

Then, as time goes by, you can gradually look for opportunities to build your network. For example, you could do the following:

- Ask colleagues, managers and clients at work and any of your volunteering opportunities.
- Chase up old professional contacts.
- When you meet professionals in real life, ask if they'd like to link up.
- Gradually build relationships with people through your real-life network and your contacts on other platforms such as Twitter.
- Ask to join up with recruiters and professionals involved in upcoming events you're attending (tell them you're looking forward to meeting them).
- Meet recruiters and professionals at events, and ask if you can join up with them (tell them you enjoyed hearing from them or meeting up).
- Join relevant LinkedIn groups such as those connected to your university, job and interests plus wider networks related to career planning, professional organisations and particular industries (use the search engine to find those related to your area, industry, or university). This will allow you to engage in conversations with other members and comment on their posts so you can gradually build a dialogue and create bonds whereby connections seem natural.
- Join up with companies' general corporate or HR pages.

When you ask to make contact with people on LinkedIn, or get in touch for any reason at all, don't use LinkedIn's template communications, but create your own personalised messages tailored to the situation and your existing relationship. Include information such as where you met, your relevant mutual contacts and the groups or organisations you have in common. For example, if you've just met someone at the rugby club, you could write:

🙶 Hi Brian. I really enjoyed meeting you with Florence after the match on Saturday – it would be great if we could link up on LinkedIn. 🙷

Using your network

While you're building up close relationships on LinkedIn, you can reach out as follows:

- Look at the career profiles of people in your chosen sector to get an idea of how you could break in.
- Use the 'Fields of study' tool to find out what other people who have the same degree as you are doing with it.
- Look up company pages and keep up with what's happening in their industries.
- Find organisations to target by location and/or industry sector.
- Participate in career-specific groups.
- Share information, and comment positively on what other people are saying, perhaps even providing a useful link or two to help out.
- Ask for informational interviews (see the earlier section on 'Five-minute chats').
- Get established contacts to put you in touch with others who may be of help.
- Wish others a happy birthday, comment on their profile updates and congratulate them on new jobs.
- Gradually build up an effective network.
- Passively sit back and let your LinkedIn profile do the talking for you when recruiters are looking for new talent (passive recruitment).

Once you've got to know people well on LinkedIn and have some good experience, there are two further ways to find jobs:

- Search the jobs database by job title, employer, location or function.
- Start asking contacts for formal work experience or internships and/or graduate positions.

Therefore, LinkedIn is a powerful career tool, but it's very much a 'slow burn'. However, this doesn't mean you should pay it scant regard at the start of your experience journey. If you want to build a network which will deliver internships and graduate jobs in the future, sign up as soon as possible and grease the wheels. Visit the site regularly, update your profile every week and stay in touch with people on an ongoing basis.

To find out more about networking on LinkedIn, see 'Using LinkedIn' on www.ed.ac.uk and 'The 31 best LinkedIn profile tips for job seekers' on www.themuse.com.

Chris Bond, Senior Recruitment Manager

The growing trend within organisations during the last three to six years has been to develop an effective in-house recruitment model. The overall goal is to reduce costs, increase the quality of applicants and gain a stronger control over how the recruitment process is executed. As a consequence, in-house recruitment and HR teams are relying more and more heavily on social media and, in particular, on LinkedIn.

Within my organisation and within my team, we use LinkedIn not only to advertise but also to search for relevant profiles, and the access we have allows us to make approaches to people we feel would be right for the vacancies we are managing. This applies to any role from the most junior entry-level positions to the most senior, and we have hiring success at all levels and within all areas, without exceptions.

My advice to all those actively involved in the job market is to ensure they have a complete profile and that it includes a picture. It does not matter if you are a recent graduate; you will still benefit from putting down all your internships and summer jobs, as the chances are that some of these will bring you up in a search. The content needs to read very closely to the way a CV would, and the most important thing is that it must contain the keywords that will be picked up by a recruiter search, and also by LinkedIn itself, so that the job ads relevant to you will be displayed when you log in. Also, your LinkedIn content is extremely visible to potential employers, so keep it professional, and do not engage in any discussions that might not show you in the best light.

Employers like to find future employees directly, and you need to give yourself every chance that they will find you.

Blogs

Blogs are personal online platforms where you can post about anything you want. They are a great way to develop a unique online presence so you stand out from the crowd, and can be especially powerful if you write well and know how to market your message via your other channels. However, you should only commit to a blog if you have the time to engage with it properly and maintain a consistently impressive product.

Some possible areas to focus on are listed here:

- Your area of interest in relation to a particular career (e.g. your love of animals if you want to be a vet).
- Your creative output (if you're an artist).
- Your situation (e.g. life as a Vietnamese student in London).
- Your experience journey (e.g. what jobs you're doing, who you're meeting, etc.).

You can set up blogs on Blogger.com and WordPress.com and find in-depth advice on www.writersdigest.com and blog.penelopetrunk.com

Other useful channels

There are numerous additional social media networks you could join, but you shouldn't get carried away, as you may lose control of your brand. In the first place, connect with people in your network and see what platforms are popular in your target industry. For example, as of late 2015, the following platforms are popular with creative students and professionals:

- Pinterest: https://www.pinterest.com
- Behance: https://www.behance.net
- Deviant Art: www.deviantart.com
- Dribbble: https://www.dribbble.com

Chapter 3

A joined-up networking strategy

The success of your networking activities comes down to three things:

- Your level of activity
- How proactive you are about making opportunities
- How you integrate your real-life and online contacts.

You can integrate your networking activities as follows:

Starting out

At the start of your networking journey, you just need to get used to meeting a wider range of people and managing your online presence:

- Decide how you want to be perceived by employers.
- Develop your personal brand accordingly – in real life and online on Facebook, Twitter and LinkedIn plus one or two other platforms that suit your style.
- Get used to all the buttons and controls on each of your social platforms.
- Make sure your brand is squeaky clean (and stays that way).
- Leave the house and meet people in a wide range of activities.
- Start joining up with people on Twitter and Facebook (if you haven't started already).
- Periodically chat to people about career-related issues in real life and on your various social media channels.

Getting deeper

Once you feel comfortable chatting about careers and managing your online presence, it's time to start taking control. Find ways to hook up with people in careers you're considering, and get involved in relevant activities such as volunteering opportunities or university societies.

You can expand your horizons as follows:

- Ask your friends, family and existing contacts to put you in touch with interesting people either in real life or on Facebook and Twitter.
- Get used to joining up with interesting people on Facebook and Twitter when you come across them either in your online conversations or in real life.
  - Expand your interactions by joining relevant organisations, social groups and societies; finding jobs and voluntary activities where

you will brush up against professionals and going to events organised by your careers service and professional organisations (such as the local Law Society).

- Join relevant groups on your social media channels, and proactively expand your network into your areas of interest.
- Get involved in any relevant activities you find on your social networks (such as employer events on campus) and keep on meeting new people.
- Manage your media channels so you keep in contact with people help them out and gradually build up closer relationships.
- Sign up to LinkedIn and connect with the better contacts you've made elsewhere.

The fast lane

Once you've built closer relationships with people, you need to build ever-more influential contacts and leverage your way into well-regarded formal opportunities and internships. You can do this by enacting the following:

- Expanding your online presence, especially on LinkedIn
- Chatting to people about their jobs
- Asking around for opportunities
- Asking contacts to put you in touch with recruiters
- Publicising your LinkedIn profile and any evidence of your work/ achievements
- Applying for jobs
- Getting help from contacts with your applications and asking them to put in a good word for you with the powers that be
- Sending off targeted speculative applications (see Chapter 9).

What if it's just not me?

If all this talk of networking and brands sends you into a cold shiver and you just want to avoid it altogether – there's some bad news and good news. The bad news is that employment is almost always, at its heart, a social endeavour, and therefore relationships will always be key. The good news is that networking need not be an ego-driven, forceful endeavour. Think of how you like to interact with people in

Chapter 3

your everyday life, and design your strategy accordingly. For example, if you just enjoy the company of work colleagues and don't go out much, look around your workplace and chat to some interesting people.

What to do now

Take a selfie and ask yourself what you represent. Then, think what you want to change to present your best self to employers (which is both fun and professional), and then get out there and start making friends. You can find out more about social networking in *Social Media for Your Student and Graduate Job Search* (Kelly, 2015).

University, societies and volunteering

Contents

Useful links

On the web

See 'Get involved' at www.volunteers.manchester.ac.uk

Search for 'volunteering' on www.prospects.ac.uk.

On Twitter

@GdnVoluntary
@joininUK
#volunteer
#Volunteering

You only get one shot

You only get one go at life, so make the most of it. Don't just attend. While you're studying (and straight afterwards), you can get involved in all manner of curricular, extra-curricular and voluntary activities which will be fun, fulfilling and good for your career prospects. Find out more throughout this chapter.

> 66 You only get one go at life, so make the most of it. 99

What you can do

In short, you can get up to almost anything at the start of your experience journey, from student societies to volunteering (or singing) in The South Pacific.

On your course

Modern university courses involve numerous opportunities to move forward in your career. You can enhance your academic skills such as research, critical thinking and analysis just by turning up and performing well in your assignments. However, you should also go the extra mile and get involved in any other skill development opportunities on offer, such as these:

- University skills awards
- Enterprise competitions

- Group-oriented modules
- Employment/enterprise/internship/volunteering-based modules
- Group activities
- Departmental/university events
- Opportunities for professional interaction.

Sandwich courses incorporating year-long internships before the final year are an absolutely unparalleled way to enhance your skills at university, improve your grades and heighten your employment opportunities. If this sounds good but you're not already on such a course, see if you can transfer. If your department and/or university doesn't offer them, talk to your tutors about teeing up some sort of personal arrangement. Find out more in Chapter 6.

Social groups at university

University students get involved in all sorts of social groups, mostly organised by the student union. They'll be listed somewhere on the Union's website along with a raft of contact details. They tend to be based around sport and other pastimes; politics and religion; particular study/career options; and popular social activities. For example, at the time of writing this guide, the University of Bath has societies focused on breakdancing, maths, finance and all things Korean plus Amnesty International, Engineers Without Borders, Buddhist Meditation, The Rugby Club and something called 'Gravity Vomit'.

Clubs in the real world

The same gamut of social groups thrives outside your university's walls in the towns, cities and villages of this great nation, you just have to do an Internet search, pop into your local library, buy your local paper or ask around. For example, in the West Midlands you can get involved with these organisations:

- The Spice Society – 'a social, adventure and activity group for ordinary people who want to do extraordinary things!'
- Mantra meditation classes
- The Chelmsley and District Conservative Club
- The Warwickshire County Cricket Club
- Your local church, mosque, synagogue, and so on.

The advantage of these non-university-based societies is that you can still attend after graduation, and they may give you access to a richer range of career contacts.

Volunteering

Volunteers work for free but their expenses are sometimes paid. Just under 20 million people in the UK formally get involved at least once a year,[1] so why don't you? You could try something connected to your personal interests or a particular career-related role. Either way, try to find opportunities that will help you enhance the specific skills you need to develop and build contacts with people who can help. For example:

- If you want to be a graphic designer, you could help out a charity with their branding.
- If you dream of becoming a patent attorney, get in touch with some legal eagles during your time at an agency such as Amnesty.

Here's how you can get started:

- Just ask interesting people and organisations if you can help out.
- Ask your department if they need any support with open days, field trips and so on.
- See if your university has a volunteering office.
- Search for 'volunteering' on your university website.
- Ask for help from your current/local HE careers service.
- Look for ideas on general student and graduate career websites such as www.prospects.ac.uk, www.thestudentroom.co.uk and www.milkround.com.
- Do an Internet search on 'volunteering in ... [your area]'.
- Attend volunteering events and fairs to see what's going on at your local careers service.
- Look at general directories such as these:
  - Bath University's Directory of Charities, Volunteering and Gap Year Opportunities at www.bath.ac.uk/careers
  - University College's extensive index at http://uclu.org/volunteering/directory

You can also find useful information and a wide range of opportunities via the following links:

- Volunteering Matters (formerly Community Service Volunteers): www.volunteeringmatters.org.uk - vacancies in social/health care, education and youth justice and many other areas.
- DirectGov: www.direct.gov.uk – search for 'Volunteering' to find lots of useful information.

Chapter 4

- Do-it: www.do-it.org.uk – search opportunities by postcode.
- Timebank: www.timebank.org.uk – volunteering focused on youth/ social issues.
- Idealist: www.idealist.org – a massive database of volunteer opportunities, jobs and internships across the globe.
- Elevation Networks: www.elevationnetworks.org – events, mentoring, internships and volunteer opportunities for students and graduates from minority ethnic backgrounds, women and those affected by a disability.
- The Guardian: http://www.theguardian.com/society/volunteering – articles and opportunities.
- i-volunteer: www.i-volunteer.org.uk – a range of interesting practical opportunities for people of any age.
- Vinspired: www.vinspired.com – volunteering website for 14- to 25-year-olds.

Susan Davies – Primary School Teacher

Unfortunately, the first time I applied for teacher training, I was knocked back. For a while I was depressed and angry, but eventually I pulled myself together.

I decided to apply the following year but, this time, I got in touch with various people to see what skills I would have to develop and demonstrate. This included course providers, careers advisers, head teachers and friends.

I concluded I'd have to get a much more practical understanding of teaching and consequently got a volunteer role in a school, twice a week, for a full year. I learnt so much, and when I applied again, I passed with flying colours.

What employers think

Recent research carried out by Reed[2] for Timebank found that:

- 73 per cent of employers prefer candidates with volunteering experience.
- 94 per cent are confident that volunteering adds to skills.
- 58 per cent believe that voluntary experience can be better for work than paid employment.

This is because, volunteering shows that you are:

- Outgoing and self-driven
- Widely experienced and skilled
- Experienced at interacting with a greater range of people
- More in control of your career than many of your peers.

However, as with most aspects of recruitment, it's quality that counts, not quantity. You won't impress anyone just by listing all the exciting and exotic things you've done at university. You need to get involved at a high level, explicitly demonstrate the specific skills you've gained and clearly relate the experience to the roles you're seeking. See how to make the most of your experience in Chapter 8.

Some ideas

Four typical student activities have been listed in the table overleaf and linked to a range of careers. Some of the opportunities are clearly linked to the occupations listed; others are just connected through the skills you could gain. This should illustrate how almost any activity can be used to your advantage in your career journey.

In the last row of the table, identify an activity you'd enjoy, the skills you could develop and how you could use the experience to move your career forward. Then – do it! You can complete the exercise right here or download it from the companion website at www.palgravecareerskills.com.

How to develop your skills

Opportunity	Some of the skills you could gain
Volunteering as a counsellor for Childline	• Empathic listening • Supporting people under pressure • Working in stressful situations • Making a commitment • Appreciating diverse needs • Getting on with children
Playing football for your student union's football society	• Fitness • Dribbling, tackling, shooting, etc. • Teamwork • Organisation (e.g. taking up a role of responsibility) • Training other people (e.g. taking up a coaching role)
Getting involved with your student union's chemistry society	• Research • Event management • Business start-up (e.g. for a scientific app) • Computer coding (e.g. for your website) • Networking (e.g. with researchers and employers)
Becoming a student representative in your department (e.g. in the Business School)	• Listening • Supporting people • Liaising with a wide range of people • Negotiating • Organisation • Solving problems
Self-assessment: Now, identify an interesting activity for yourself	
What you could do	Skills you could develop (avoid jargon)

How each of these experiences could be used to boost your career in various sectors

Counselling: Reflect on your counselling experience to see if this is the career for you, and demonstrate this understanding to get onto a course.
Medicine/nursing: Voluntary counselling can help you get into more clinical positions such as a role as a care assistant which will, in turn, help you get onto your training course.
Law: Develop your ability to listen carefully and extract information in high-pressure situations with a wide range of clients.

Football coaching: This activity would give you a deeper understanding of the needs of players and access to contacts and training courses.
Marketing: Develop your teamwork skills in all sorts of situations and get involved with campaigns to raise funds.
Civil service: Take up a position of responsibility to develop your organisation and written communications skills.

Pharmaceutical sales: Organise some sort of drug-related research and take the opportunity to meet up with representatives of drug companies.
Web design for a technical organisation: Develop web pages for your society on your favourite technical issues.
Accountancy: Organise activities and events related to non-technical careers/meet up with accountants in scientific companies.

Electronic engineering: Develop your liaison skills, so you can show employers how you will interact with colleagues and clients.
Sales: Reflect on how you successfully negotiate and persuade, so you can demonstrate these skills in your applications.
Investment banking: Use your access to influential academics and administrators in your department to connect with industry professionals.

Your Experience

Some ideas on how you could make the most of what you do

Chapter 4

What to do now

The wonderful freedom of volunteering is that you can do whatever you want. So, start by simply closing your eyes and dreaming of some exciting activities. Then, get involved.

Emily Connor – President, SHU Student Union

Student activities are constantly growing, depending on the needs and ability of our students, ranging from societies to sports, volunteering and social enterprise. The benefit that is constantly mentioned is that these activities will make you, as a student, more employable, stretching your skills and personal development. However, whilst this is entirely true and crucial, they also have the capacity for so much more than that!

For me personally, getting involved in my Student Union kept me in University when I was struggling to cope with moving away from home. I didn't particularly get on with my housemates, or have many friends on my course, but joining a society and volunteering *made* my time at university. The friends I made and the cultures I was exposed to helped me think in new ways that not only aided my degree, but also my development as a person. Joining societies helped to develop my passions and interests; being on committees enabled me to become a leader; and being a representative helped to develop my own politics. From there I ran in the Student Union elections and have had the honour of representing students at Sheffield Hallam for 2 years.

My journey started by braving it to an Activities Fair during Freshers' Week and culminated in me running for Student Union president. Others found inspiration in volunteering for their future career or networked their way to their dream job. Others made friends for life and have travelled abroad as a result or did some incredible things for charity, developing their skills to be ready for graduation. Everyone's journey is different, but equally as important. Therefore, engagement in student activities isn't just fun or developmental. It's transformative.

Chapter 5

Part-time, temporary and full-time work

Contents

Useful links

On the web

See 'Why temping is tempting' at www.theguardian.com

See 'Working part time' at www. thecompleteuniversityguide.co.uk

www.student-jobs.co.uk

www.e4s.co.uk

On Twitter

@studentjobsUK

@Guardianjobs

#UKjobs

#jobsearch

Hi ho, hi ho

Work is increasingly becoming an integral part of normal student life. According to a recent student survey from The Students Union and Endsleigh,[1] 59 per cent of full-time students hold down a job, 46 per cent on a part-time basis and 13 per cent full-time.

This chapter provides an outline of tasks you can undertake, how much work you should do, the benefits and where you can find the best opportunities.

What you can do

Temping

One traditional work option for students has always been temporary work – either part-time during the term and/or full-time in the vacations. Typical posts have usually been in areas such as the service sector, telesales and office work, but opportunities have recently diversified into every sector.

Seasonal jobs

Many organisations recruit students over certain periods such as Christmas and summer. For example The Royal Mail and many larger retailers tend to recruit extra staff from November onwards, and children's/sporting activity groups often take on extra staff over July and August. Some seasonal job agencies and job boards are listed later in this chapter.

Permanent (ongoing) roles

Of course, work experience isn't just reserved for the two weeks you spend at the local hairdressers in year 12. It's a lifelong process. Therefore, in a sense, every job you ever get will be employment experience, even if you're working full-time. If you're lucky, you could get a job in the exact career you want to enter, but any ongoing position could help you in several ways. For example, you could do the following:

- Fit a part-time, permanent role around your study.
- Work full-time and study part-time.
- Take a year off from uni.
- Build up your CV and pay your bills once you've graduated.
- Get your foot in the door of an organisation or sector.
- Change careers once you've already started a graduate role.

An increasing number of students already have permanent jobs when they arrive at university or gradually work their way into ongoing roles once they're on campus.

Deirdre Blewitt, mature student

As a 49-year-old divorced mother of three, I am beyond excited to have completed year 1 of my BSc Counselling & Psychotherapy course. I had been brought to this juncture by many life experiences, some challenging and sad, others exciting and growth-producing.

My first useful experience of counselling was the months of intensive counselling I underwent to deal with a dysfunctional marriage, which provided me with a safe and peaceful environment to work through my hurt, pain and confusion, and helped me eventually reach the decision to divorce my husband.

My work life also pointed me in the direction of counselling as a career. Fifteen years working as a library assistant in my local library has certainly been a fantastic foundation and ground to set the seed for this new career. I spent many happy hours chatting to borrowers and being their confidant on particular challenges in their life as we searched for the perfect book to support their transitions in work and personal lives. Now I get to continue on this investigative journey in a more in-depth and fulfilling way.

The pros and cons of working at uni

A job will allow you to:

- Pay the bills
- Minimise your student debt
- Live a more fulfilling existence

- Develop your skills
- Get experience for your CV
- Make useful contacts

However, the picture isn't entirely rosy. Too much work can also hold you back. This is primarily because you'll have less time to study and rest. It would be a totally false economy to pay thousands of pounds for a degree only to perform poorly because you're too busy earning the minimum wage. Also, although employers will typically respect you for sticking at a job, the opportunities for skill development may be limited (there are only so many ways you can deliver a pizza).

Furthermore, too much work is bound to limit the time you can spend on other activities such as clubs, volunteering and internships (too much work makes Jack a dull boy). Therefore, you need to find some sort of equilibrium whereby you can gain the advantages of working but also engage in other worthwhile activities.

However, whatever you do, don't miss lectures or assignments because of your workload. If you're in doubt about whether you're working too much, you probably are. In this case, consult your tutors or a careers adviser and ask for advice.

Universities tend to suggest that students should limit their work commitments to about 15 to 17 hours a week. However, Oxford and Cambridge reputedly suggest that you shouldn't work at all.

Chapter 5

What employers think

Employers are very attracted to paid employment experience because they highly rate the skills you gain on the job. They also value the commitment you demonstrate to hold down a position and the maturity to manage your own career.

So, where are the jobs?

Students are intelligent, resourceful and cheap so you can be very attractive to employers. A wide range of job sources is outlined below. You should also be able to find many opportunities through your networks (see Chapter 3).

Social networks

Keep on top of your social media channels as more and more student opportunities are being advertised on these platforms. Twitter is a great source of opportunities across the board – just find the relevant recruitment and industry usernames and hashtags in your chosen sector, and keep your eyes open. LinkedIn also has a great database for more formal experience opportunities, internships and graduate roles at www.linkedin.com/studentjobs.

On the high street

Back in the day, if you wanted to find work or any sort of voluntary experience, you needed a good pair of shoes, a bag full of CVs and a map. You'd pop into every shop, warehouse, theatre, bingo hall (ask your mum) and office with a smile on your face and ask if they were hiring. Your chances of success at each interaction were small, but the more people you saw, the luckier you got. Surprisingly, this approach still bears fruit today, especially with less formal roles, as it shows enterprise, drive and good communication.

At first, it can be challenging just walking up to employers and trying your luck, but you'll soon get the hang of it. Try to avoid nervously handing over your CV and running out with your tail between your legs. Chat to the people you see about their jobs, try to speak to the manager or someone in charge and don't forget to get some contact details before you leave so you can follow up and say thanks.

Shop windows

Many local shops still have noticeboards promoting opportunities, for example:

- Corner shops may have adverts for local jobs such as cleaners and shop assistants.
- Specialist retailers, such as music shops, may be able to put you in touch with people who are looking for skilled people in their particular sector.

Newspapers and magazines

Newspapers, magazines and trade publications still carry job ads, plus they can be really useful sources of news and information about future vacancies. For example, if *The Stage* reports that more actors may soon be needed to act as patients with particular illnesses for medical students. You could make contact with the relevant training managers on LinkedIn or give them a call. The Guardian's recruitment pages are especially useful; see www.jobs.theguardian.com

Job boards

A myriad of organisations advertise general temporary, permanent, part-time and full-time jobs, including these:

- Fish4Jobs: www.fish4.co.uk/jobs
- Jobsite: www.jobsite.co.uk
- Total Jobs: www.totaljobs.com
- Monster: www.monster.co.uk
- Student Job: www.studentjob.co.uk
- LeisureJobs: www.leisurejobs.com

Agencies

The UK has a wealth of excellent recruitment agencies. Some national chains (including those listed below) offer vacancies across the board. Others focus on specific regions and sectors. Find some that suit you at https://www.rec.uk.com. Local papers also usually list agencies in each town, and your careers service will probably be able to recommend the best local firms. Furthermore, your university may well have a 'job shop', and finally, don't forget Jobcentre Plus at https://www.direct. gov.uk. Some of the larger national agencies are shown below.

A handful of UK agencies (find more on https://www.rec.com)

- Michael Page: www.michaelpage.co.uk – diverse vacancies in roles from accountancy to retail and life sciences.
- Reed: www.reed.co.uk – another giant with a similarly wide remit and good career planning/job-hunting advice.
- Blue Arrow: www.bluearrow.co.uk – office work and vacancies in practical areas such as catering and industry.
- Hays: www.hays.co.uk – jobs in a massive range of sectors, from casual to executive, plus good job-hunting advice.
- Office Angels: www.office-angels.com – secretarial and office support and a gradually broadening range of opportunities.

Sian Jenkins, student

When I started at university, I tried to sign up with a few agencies but they said I needed more experience, which seemed strange because that's why I wanted to work for them in the first place! However, I got a voluntary job in a local charity and improved my typing speed using an online programme.

When I tried to sign up again, three agencies took me on but never got in touch so I was starting to take things personally! This time I asked around to see who everyone else worked for and the same agency kept on being mentioned. A friend of mine said she'd refer me, so I gave them my details and hey presto! I've been working for them ever since.

Many agencies look for people with specific employment experience and competencies such as the ability to type more than 50 words per minute or mix concrete (but not usually both!). You'll probably need to develop these skills in other voluntary or paid roles before applying. Some agencies which focus on holiday jobs in the UK are shown below (sources for holiday jobs overseas can be found in Chapter 7):

- Indeed: www.indeed.co.uk/Seasonal-jobs – temporary posts in a wide range of sectors.

- E4s.co.uk: www.e4s.co.uk – holiday jobs/long-term positions.
- Summer-jobs.co.uk: www.summer-jobs.co.uk – activity-based roles throughout the year.

Be careful when you sign up for agencies. Don't pay a registration fee; make sure the websites are regularly updated; and, above all, if no work is forthcoming, move on. Finally, remember: the lowest salary you say you'll consider will be the highest you'll ever be offered.

University careers services

Careers services tend to advertise experience opportunities formally on their websites and informally through word of mouth and their social networks.

Professional organisations

Professional organisations are a good source of industry-specific news and 'hidden' vacancies. For example, The Chartered Society for Designers at www.csd.org.uk lists agencies and vacancies and offers a 'find a designer' service.

Individual organisations

Take some time to bookmark the websites of the specific firms where you'd like to work, and keep abreast of what's going on. This will not only highlight any vacancies but also help you prepare for any future employment trends.

Search engines

Why not spend half an hour a week searching on terms such as 'jobs in catering', 'volunteer marketing positions' or 'seasonal jobs'?

Some ideas

As in the previous chapter, the table overleaf links some typical student opportunities (this time, jobs) to a range of careers. Reflect on how these experiences can be positively used in any career journey, and this time identify a possible job for yourself, list the skills you'd gain and outline how you could use your experiences to further your career. You can complete the exercise right here or download it from the companion website at www.palgravecareerskills.com.

How to develop your skills

Opportunity	Some of the skills you could gain
Working part-time as a sales assistant	<ul><li>Customer service</li><li>Management (e.g. becoming a supervisor)</li><li>Commercial awareness</li><li>Marketing (e.g. designing a sales campaign)</li></ul>
Working part-time as a paralegal	<ul><li>Legal research</li><li>Informational interviewing</li><li>Efficient work practices</li><li>Organisation</li><li>Liaison with clients</li><li>Commercial awareness</li><li>Working under pressure</li></ul>
A full-time post as a restaurant manager (and either studying part-time or fitting your hours around your study)	<ul><li>Customer service</li><li>Commercial awareness</li><li>Leadership</li><li>Managing resources</li><li>Balancing a multitude of tasks</li><li>Innovation (e.g. designing a new menu)</li><li>Drive</li></ul>
Working over your Easter and summer vacations at a children's camp	<ul><li>Working with children</li><li>Teaching</li><li>Organisation</li><li>Managing your time</li><li>Leadership</li><li>Patience</li></ul>

Self-assessment: Now, identify an interesting activity for yourself	
What you could do	Skills you could develop (avoid jargon)

How each of these experiences could be used to boost your career in various sectors

Retail management: Develop relevant skills and contacts plus a deep understanding of the sector you can demonstrate in your applications.
Officer in the army: Reflect on how you motivate colleagues and maintain morale in difficult circumstances.
Politics: Engage with group activities such as staff committees and trade union events.

Solicitor: Develop skills for a particular legal sector, make contacts and gradually move sideways into a training contract (either before or after you start your legal training).
Accountant: Identify the specific skills required by the firms you're targeting and get used to demonstrating them in your daily tasks.
Teaching: Find opportunities to develop and demonstrate your skills of organisation, efficiency, professionalism and capacity for hard work.

Hospitality management: Look for opportunities to develop the particular skills and contacts you'll need in the specific sector you're targeting.
Scientific laboratory technician: Focus on the skills you've developed as a manager such as organisation, and management of resources.
Setting up your own B&B: Transfer your understanding of the sector and get in touch with experts to help you develop a successful business.

Social work: Get used to helping children out with specific difficulties and demonstrate how you did this in your applications for further study.
Surveyor: Look for outstanding opportunities to develop the full range of transferable skills required by most employers (see Chapter 1).
Educational psychologist: Look for opportunities to improve and demonstrate the skills you'll need in your career such as empathic listening, assessing needs and applying effective interventions.

Your Experience

Some ideas on how you could make the most of what you do

Chapter 5

Tax and National Insurance

Unfortunately, in the words of Benjamin Franklin, 'Nothing is certain in life except death and taxes.'[2] So, when you start your first job, the employer will complete a 'Starter Checklist' to work out your tax code (the level of tax they will deduct). Subsequently, each time you leave a job, you will be given a form called a P45 which you can take to new employers.

Once the paperwork has been sorted out, your employer will then take income tax and National Insurance (NI) out of your wages before you're even paid. However, the good news is that in the current tax system (as this book goes to print), you'll only start paying tax on your earnings over about £200/week or £900/month, and NI on weekly earnings over about £150. You can check exact current tax thresholds at https://www.gov.uk/student-jobs-paying-tax.

Make sure your tax paperwork has been sorted as soon as you start each new job, or you may end up paying emergency tax at a higher rate than you should – and it can be a real pain getting it back. You will also need to give your employer your National Insurance number. You should have automatically got this just before your 16th birthday, but if you don't have it, contact the National Insurance Helpline at https://www.gov.uk/national-insurance.

Students from the European Union (EU), The European Economic Area (EEA) and Switzerland (the full list of countries is listed below) have the right to work in the UK; however, there are currently some extra requirements for Bulgarians, Romanians and Croatians, and the rules regularly change. Find out the current situation at www.ukba.homeoffice.gov.uk. International students from outside these regions often have limited work privileges – see www.ukcisa. org.uk.

As with everybody else, international students and those from the EU, EEA and Switzerland need a National Insurance number, which you can get through the dedicated National Insurance pages for non-UK residents at https://www.gov.uk. You will also need to show your passport and visa to your employer when you sign up for work.

Helen Caunce, Commissioning Editor

I'd worked on a student magazine at university and thought that publishing could suit my interests. To find out more about what the job of an editor involves, I looked up some local companies and found details of editors who worked there, then sent a message to see if anyone would meet me. One person got back to me, and I went to her office to hear more about what her job is like. The meeting was really positive, and so I started emailing companies to ask for work experience. Two companies got back to me, and I ended up with placements at both publishing houses. Initially, I was quite worried about being rejected, and it took a couple of weeks before I heard back from anyone. That was quite a nerve-wracking time. I'd say that persistence is really important if you want to find interesting work experience.

What to do now

Get stuck in. You don't need to find the best job, just one that pays the bills. You can then move on when better opportunities turn up.

Chapter 5

Countries whose citizens have an automatic right to work in the UK (as of January 2015)

The European Union
Austria, Belgium, Bulgaria*, Croatia*, Republic of Cyprus, Czech Republic, Denmark, Estonia, Finland, France, Germany, Greece, Hungary, Ireland, Italy, Latvia, Lithuania, Luxembourg, Malta, the Netherlands, Poland, Portugal, Romania*, Slovakia, Slovenia, Spain, Sweden and the UK

The European Economic Area
Iceland, Liechtenstein and Norway

Additional countries
Switzerland

* Citizens from these countries may be subject to restrictions.

Chapter 6

Internships and placements

Contents

Useful links

On the web

See 'Work experience' at www.prospects.ac.uk

See 'How to find an internship' at www.birmingham.ac.uk

Look up 'Internships and work experience' at www.ed.ac.uk

www.ratemyplacement.co.uk

On LinkedIn

www.linkedin.com/studentjobs

On Twitter

#UKinternship

#ukjobs

The cream of the crop

Well-managed internships and placements are the best experience you can get.

What are internships?

Cambridge Dictionaries Online defines internships as 'periods of time during which someone works for a company or organisation in order to get experience of a particular type of work'.[1] Traditionally, they range in length from two weeks to a year (usually a month or two) and involve some form of professional instruction and reflection. It is this training aspect that makes them so valuable for both students and employers. Therefore, they've been used by major recruiters in the UK for a very long time. However, their use has recently expanded and diversified in terms of their length, what's involved, the training and support provided and their practical relevance. Therefore, with some internships you'll still get valuable experience and feedback, but with others, you'll just be told to clean the office and make the tea. So, you need to carefully seek out respected projects which are linked to your academic study, experience and skills as well as what you want to do in your career.

Why they've taken off

In 2013, the top 100 organisations advertised 11,819 paid internships.[2] However, this is just the tip of the iceberg as thousands more are offered each year across the spectrum. Internships have become so popular because:

- They allow recruiters to appraise candidates' skills in real work situations over extended periods of time
- They can help you contextualise your study
- They're widespread in other countries
- Skilled students and graduates are aplenty
- All experience is increasingly being called 'internships'
- Interns are cheap (and often free).

Paid or unpaid

Interns have traditionally received a small stipend, but increasingly, you'll be expected to work for free. For example, in August 2014, the Social Mobility and Child Poverty Commission found that 83 per cent of new entrants to journalism undertake internships, and 92 per cent of these are unpaid.[3] This is okay for students and graduates who can rely on parental assistance and someone to put them up. However, if you can't support yourself without a paid job or take time off work, then internships may seem totally untenable. Nonetheless, you can adopt several strategies to help you compete:

- Move to where the internships are (often London)
- Get an evening/weekend job to free up your days
- Build up contacts so you can couch-surf (Facebook your third cousin removed, your girlfriend's brother's friends, etc.)
- Save up some money
- Look for opportunities which are relatively short in length.

What you can do

Nowadays, internships and placements are offered in most sectors. Specific firms usually offer opportunities in certain fields and seek students and/or graduates from particular disciplines. For example, a particular engineering firm may want science/engineering students

Chapter 6

for a technical project, and a media company may ask for skills in marketing. However, big companies also need experts in all sectors from HR to marketing, PR and logistics.

Insight programmes

These are short, introductory programmes offered by investment banks and other graduate employers, which last anything from a day to a week around Easter. They are traditionally offered to first-year students but many firms are now opening up their doors to students and graduates at any level, as long as you have enough UCAS points (usually about 300). Exceptional talent is often identified early on and fast-tracked onto assessment centres for internships in later years. Therefore, these short experience opportunities are a great way to get noticed. For example, the global financial services company, PwC recently advertised the following open day on its careers website at www.pwc.co.uk/careers.

PwC Entry Route Career Open Days – Technology

Location: National

Business Area: Work experience – all business areas

Closing Date: You can apply for this vacancy all year round, but to avoid disappointment, we'd advise you to apply as early as you can. Open to all undergraduates and graduates, our Technology Career open day is a one-day course to experience hands-on business simulations and high-level case studies. Discover hints and tips on our recruitment process, as well as gain an opportunity to get a taste of what it's like to work at PwC.

With a day packed full of interactive challenges and some exciting insights about technology at PwC, we'll cover everything from IT strategy, architecture and design to enterprise applications, sourcing, project management and IT operations.

That, in a nutshell, is what Technology at PwC is all about. You'll also get to speak with our people in Technology roles during a panel session. And with four different areas to choose from, you're bound to find something to fit you perfectly: Forensic Technology Solutions; HR Technology; Technology Assurance; Technology Consulting

Traditional internships and placements

Most of the major recruiters in the UK traditionally hire student interns for 10 weeks or so during the summer vacation, just before they go back to university for their final year of study. These programmes are usually very well organised and structured to give you a taste of the different roles and recruitment streams on offer within each particular organisation. These positions also still tend to come with a decent salary. Therefore, they're very popular.

Larger UK graduate employers increasingly use traditional internships as their main way of identifying future talent. In fact, the 2014 High Fliers Survey found that about half the graduate roles at the major blue-chip companies are now reserved for interns,[4] and some companies have even stopped looking for graduates altogether. Students are attracted for the following reasons:

- The fact that internships look very good on a CV or application form
- The professional training
- The money in the bank
- The chance of being fast-tracked into a graduate role after university.

Melissa Hughes, recent graduate

Take the time to find a role in the organisation that fits you best, then work hard to prove yourself. In this way, interesting avenues will soon open up. Don't worry if you make mistakes, but try to learn from them, and don't be afraid to ask questions.

The details of a typical summer internship at Nestlé are shown below. This information was downloaded from www.nestlecareers.co.uk in

January 2015. Of course, the internships at this firm may differ by the time you're reading this book, and salaries may go up or down (hopefully, the former).

Summer Placements at the Nestlé Academy

Learn about the world of Fast Moving Consumer Goods (FMCG) and develop valuable skills that will help further your career.

Our Summer Internship programme offers the chance to get hands-on experience in the world's leading nutrition, health and wellness company. It will introduce you to a potential future work environment and allow you to test your interest in a particular career before making permanent commitments. Furthermore, you'll develop skills in applying theory to practical work situations.

You'll join the company in our York or Gatwick offices or in one of the factories around the UK and Ireland. We offer a range of internship types, including Sales, Marketing, Manufacturing, Safety, Health and Environment (SHE), HR and Finance. The programme takes place for 10 weeks over the summer – from the end of June to the end of August. During this time, you'll be assigned a relevant project or set of objectives that you'll work on under the mentorship of your allocated line manager. The work you'll be assigned will have real value to the business. At the end of your internship, you'll present your results and recommendations to senior managers and your team.

Relevant training will be provided during an induction period. This could consist of one-on-one talks with people across your department or training day sessions regarding Nestlé's vision, values and policies. Depending on the function you join, you'll also have training in presentation, negotiation and sales skills.

This internship is ideal to take in the summer before your final year of university as it's a great opportunity to prove yourself as a suitable candidate for the graduate programme. You'll be paid a rate of £16,500 pro rata over the 10-week period.

Modern internships

Over the last few years, numerous new internships have appeared alongside the traditional opportunities outlined above. They are typically less structured and more flexible in terms of length, who can sign up, the level of training and payment.

These roles are often accessible to both students and graduates. In fact, many of them now gather multiple internships on their CVs as they strive to get noticed.

Stephen Walsh, Warehouse Supervisor

When I graduated with a degree in economics a few years ago, I travelled and then came back thinking I'd go straight back into work; however, this didn't happen. I ended up staying at home and getting increasingly angry with my family and life in general. However, luckily my dad got me an internship at a warehouse where a friend of his worked (he wanted to get rid of me!). I was dubious about doing a manual job after going to university, but I gave it a shot. Luckily, the job opened up my eyes. I realised there was much more to work than I'd assumed, and I got stuck into so many fun projects, making friends as I went along.

Unfortunately, there was no job at the end of the internship, but it didn't really matter too much because the important thing was that I felt re-energised. I asked around the office before I left, and someone put me in touch with an agency in the sector. My boss gave me a great reference, and I was back at work in no time in another 2-month internship. This time, a proper job came through, and I'm now in a great role as a warehouse supervisor in the retail industry.

Sandwich placements

These are the gold standard of internships and may also be called 'industrial placements', 'year-long internships', 'placement years', 'years in industry' and numerous other terms. They are rated highly by students and academics because they offer opportunities to:

- Undertake substantial experience.
- Develop excellent technical and transferable skills.
- Make influential contacts.
- Be seriously considered for a graduate role (up to 70 per cent of students undertaking placements are subsequently employed).
- Be 4.6 per cent more likely to gain a first and 6 per cent more likely to achieve a 2:1 than non-placement students.
- Earn anything from £150,000 to £25,000 (higher in London and the South East). (Information from the Association for Sandwich Education and Training (ASET)).[5]

These year-long placements are typically undertaken as part of sandwich courses just before the final year of study. Students usually remain registered on their courses and pay fees (although these are often reduced). In return, your department usually helps you find a position (although it will be down to you at the end of the day). They also support you throughout your time away from campus, especially in terms of:

- Pre-placement training in areas such as finding a position and completing effective applications.
- Formal reflection on your personal development during and after your time at work.

Before your chosen placement is approved, your department will have to make sure it is legal and ethical. In most cases, this shouldn't be a problem.

These placements are a fantastic way to network with employers, develop invaluable experience and improve your subject understanding and grades. Furthermore, a large proportion of placement students are subsequently hired full-time.

If you're not on a sandwich degree, there's every chance you'll still be able to undertake a year in industry before you start your final year on campus. You'll have to be more proactive with placement providers, administrators and academics at your institution, but your initiative should be recognised and applauded. Get in touch with the placement/employability tutor in your department and your careers service as soon as possible to see what they can do.

Over the next two pages, you'll find an advert for a year in industry placement at National Grid (taken from www.ratemyplacement. co.uk in January 2015) and excellent advice from Sarah Tomlinson at Coventry University.

Find out how to maximise the benefits of a sandwich placement in Chapter 8.

Technical Engineering Industrial Placement at National Grid

Our Student Development Programme offers you a fantastic insight into a number of career paths within National Grid that are crucial to its future successes.

A 12-month industrial placement is offered during your penultimate year at university.

Best of all if you have delivered excellent performance during your placements you will be offered an opportunity on our Graduate Development Programme at the start of your final year, leaving your free to concentrate on achieving that all-important grade.

Career Area
We have opportunities across a number of areas within National Grid, such as:

- Market Operations – Electricity Operations
- Market Operations – Gas Operations
- Market Operations – Commercial Operations
- Gas Distribution – Operations
- Gas Distribution – Network Strategy.

Degrees Required

- Market Operations – on target to achieve a 2:2 or above in Electrical, Electrical & Electronic or Electrical & Mechanical Engineering
- Gas Distribution – on target to achieve a 2:2 or above in Mechanical, Electrical or Civil Engineering.

Chapter 6

Chapter 6

Sarah Tomlinson, Student Placement Advisor

You need more than only your degree subject knowledge when entering the graduate market; you need relevant work experience. A sandwich placement year is especially valuable.

Use your first year of your degree to gain various types of experience; this can be a regular part-time job in a local restaurant, a part-time job relevant to your course, a summer placement, any kind of volunteering, joining a society at your university or taking part in extracurricular activities. All of these activities will enhance your transferable skills and therefore how employable you are on paper. During your first year of your degree, also make sure you see your university careers/employment tutors to help you develop your CV to a high standard.

Once you enter your second year of study, you will be ready to apply for sandwich placements. During this year, again make sure you see your careers/employment tutors for assistance. Most universities will bring employers onto campus for presentations about their placement schemes or the industry itself. Make sure you are attending as many employability workshops and presentations as possible; they are designed to help you understand the industry, the working environment, that particular company and what they want to see from good candidates on their application forms.

During your placement year, most companies will allow you to go on relevant training courses to further develop your skills; embrace these opportunities! Work hard and impress your managers, and you may be offered a part-time position so you can continue to work there whilst you complete your final year of study or even a graduate position on completion of your placement year.

If you are able to apply yourself in this way throughout your university life, you will put yourself in a good starting position for the graduate career you are seeking.

Internships for specific groups

A number of private, public and third-sector organisations offer targeted internships for people from particular sectors of society who have particular difficulties and/or are unfairly represented.

Some people from disadvantaged groups can feel awkward about taking up these internships because they don't feel comfortable about being labelled and receiving charity. However, rest assured, the groups that organise these opportunities are focused on addressing inequality of opportunity, that is redressing the negative pressures already placed on particular groups, not just giving them special attention. You will also receive excellent training attuned to your specific needs and contacts for which most people would give an arm or a leg.

Finding vacancies

First come, first served

Employers tend to advertise their internships and placements well in advance and start looking at applications as soon as they come in. Therefore, don't wait for the closing date to make contact. Look for new opportunities every day, and apply as soon as they appear.

The major recruiters tend to start advertising insight programmes, traditional internships or placements and 12-month opportunities in September, the year before the positions actually commence. Most of these vacancies will be filled well before Christmas, but keep your eyes open right into spring and summer, because some larger organisations and many smaller ones will be slow off the mark. The modern internships outlined above also peak in autumn but increasingly tend to be offered year round.

Whatever you do, don't wait until the last moment before applying, as it takes time to get your applications in order. Get ready for your full-on assault during your summer break, and get stuck in as soon as the vacancies start appearing. That way you'll have your choice of positions before anyone else has even put pen to paper.

Where to look

Specific organisations Keep track of all the websites and social networks for firms where you'd like to work and see what comes up.

General student and graduate career websites Although these websites focus primarily on permanent graduate jobs, they also carry a wide range of placements and internships. Try the following links:

- Prospects: www.prospects.ac.uk

- Milkround: www.milkround.com
- TARGETjobs: www.targetjobs.co.uk
- Inside Careers: www.insidecareers.co.uk.

Your department Academics and administrators in your faculty may formally and informally advertise relevant opportunities, especially if they run sandwich degrees. Get in touch with your placement tutor as soon as possible, and get as much help as you can.

Specific internship websites A number of outstanding organisations target this new market, such as those listed here:

- Ratemyplacement: www.ratemyplacement.co.uk – an excellent site with jobs, advice and reviews on all kinds of student and graduate internships.
- Inspiring Interns: www.inspiringinterns.com – another popular site with vacancies, advice and a CV drop box.
- InternTown: www.interntown – internships across the globe including many in the UK.
- Graduate Talent Pool: https://graduatetalentpool.gov.uk – the Government's own job board for graduates who want to take up internships, covering a wide range of opportunities, primarily in England.
- TopInternships: www.topinternships.com – an interesting site with good advice and news sections.
- STEP: www.step.org.uk – well-regarded organisation which arranges project-based internships, including short-term undergraduate work placements, sandwich placements and graduate internships.
- Your university: Many universities themselves now also run internship programmes for students and/or graduates. Just ask your careers service.

Your social networks Keep on top of the usernames and hashtags where vacancies are advertised for students in your sector, such as @GradCracker for engineering and technology jobs and #charityjobs for positions in charities. You can find some relevant addresses and advice at www.social-hire.com, but you should already be connected with all the best tweeters in your sector (see Chapter 3).

However, as far as internships go, LinkedIn is the king at this stage in your career journey, so you should also be a master of this wonderful networking tool. You can pick up jobs by networking, sitting back and waiting for employers to contact you and reaching out via www. linkedin.com/studentjobs.

General work experience websites These websites focus on experience of all kinds including internships:

- E4s.co.uk: www.e4s.co.uk
- Student Ladder: www.studentladder.co.uk
- GoThinkBig: www.gothinkbig.co.uk.

Job agencies/Boards Some of the larger agencies and job boards in the UK that advertise internships are listed below. You can find more local agencies on the website of The Recruitment and Employment Confederation at www.rec.uk.com.

- Total Jobs: www.totaljobs.com
- Indeed: www.indeed.co.uk
- Fish4jobs: www.fish4.co.uk/jobs
- Gradplus: www.gradplus.com
- Reed: www.reed.co.uk
- Jobsite: www.jobsite.co.uk
- The Guardian job site: www.jobs.theguardian.com.

University careers service/Job agencies Keep track of what appears on your relevant university websites, but also pop in to find less formal opportunities. Other universities' vacancy websites may also not be password-protected. For example, as of January 2015, the internships advertised by The Careers Group at the University of London are publicly available: www.jobonline. thecareersgroup.co.uk.

Charities and special interest groups Look at websites devoted to your particular needs to find relevant experience opportunities. For example, as of late 2014:

- Fidelity Worldwide Investment: www.fidelityrecruitment.com – offers a Women's Investment Insight Week for women from any academic background (primarily first-year degree students).

- The Windsor Fellowship: www.windsor-fellowship.org – offers a 'Leadership Programme' for second-year undergraduates from a black or minority ethnic group.
- The Royal National Institute of Blind People (RNIB) Scotland: www.rnib.org.uk – offers internships to school, college and university leavers who are blind or partially sighted and live north of the border.

If you don't have the grades

Many of the larger graduate recruiters stipulate that applicants should have certain grades such as 300 UCAS points and/or a 2:1 (or the expectation of such).

If you don't have (or expect) these grades, you'll definitely have fewer options, but don't despair – you just need to be more strategic. Don't just send off hundreds of applications and hope you'll still be considered because you're so impressive in every other area of life – you won't. You'll probably be rejected by a computer before a human even sees what you've written.

One tactic is to get in touch with the relevant HR professionals at organisations and ask them to consider your applications, notwithstanding your poor grades. You should give good reasons why your qualifications aren't quite up to scratch (such as a death in the family or an illness) and stress your unique strengths. There's usually some sort of email address/phone number or social networking address on applications, but try to contact a manager who has the power to make decisions. Managers' contact details can usually be found on LinkedIn, and they often visit campuses from October onwards.

If this approach doesn't bear fruit, you can also:

- Build effective contacts with influential people in organisations who may be able to get your applications past the initial sift. You can do this online or in real life, for example at your cousin's bar mitzvah or when employers visit your university.
- Focus on organisations that don't stipulate good grades, such as many smaller and medium-sized businesses.

- Go for less competitive internships in your chosen industry, just to get your foot in the door.
- Get creative: think of clever ways to get in (see the advice in Chapter 8).

Don't forget to dream

There are numerous paths into every career, and almost any experience can be useful if managed in the right way, so don't feel limited by traditional options. For example, if you're planning on becoming a nurse, you could look for a role in a care home like everyone else or get a job providing first aid on an oil rig, support travellers on a pilgrimage or help out at a Premiership rugby club. The world is your oyster! The advantage of looking for roles you'll truly enjoy is that your passion and excitement will mark you out as an excellent candidate, and you'll get far more out of the experience. Consider what 'floats your boat' in the exercise below. You can complete the exercise right here or download it from the companion website at www.palgravecareerskills.com.

Self-assessment: Your dream internships

1 Close your eyes and dream of an amazing internship (dream big!).
2 Find one that matches.

Your dream internship	Actual internships that match

Reflecting on your answers: Are you struggling to come up with ideas? If this is the case, are you really allowing yourself to dream? Get away from your room at home or uni, take a walk and visualise an amazing experience!

What to do now

Get out there and start applying! Sometimes people don't start looking for formal experience opportunities just because they don't want to risk rejection. However, if you don't give it a go, you'll never get that wonderful feeling of facing up to your challenges and finding a fulfilling role.

Heading overseas

Contents

- She's got a ticket to ride
- The pros and cons
- Visas and permission to work
- Finding somewhere to live
- Volunteering
- Working
- Some ideas
- What to do now

Useful links

On the web

See 'Gap Year' 100 company directory at www.telegraph.co.uk

See 'Gap Year' at www.prospects.ac.uk

See 'Top 10 tips to surviving an internship abroad' at www.vergemagazine.com

On LinkedIn

www.linkedin.com/studentjobs

On Facebook

Sign up for the group: 'Backpacking'

She's got a ticket to ride

The world is getting smaller, and students and graduates are increasingly keen to get experience overseas. This includes a quarter of a million brave souls who leave our shores every year on some sort of gap year.[1]

Almost all the experience you can gain here in the UK is also available overseas – and much more to boot. However, many people hesitate because the logistics can be daunting and the road uncertain. But you shouldn't let your fears get in the way – it can be a wonderful experience and you'll definitely get out what you put in. The tricky issues primarily revolve around language, costs, finding opportunities, accommodation, visas, travel, safety and value for money. The good news is your English skills and enterprise will be in high demand, especially if you have some knowledge of the local language and culture.

The next chapter deals with issues related to getting the most out of work, as well as safety and value for money, but you can find advice and guidance on all the other relevant issues right here. As usual, please note that the links provided throughout this chapter are just a selection of what's out there, so you should see them as a launching point for your wider research.

The pros and cons

As stressed throughout this guide, all experience is good, but overseas work and travel can mark you out as a special talent. This is because it is widely recognised as a great way to enhance your skills, commitment and knowledge. For example, you may develop the following:

- Extra transferable skills such as foreign languages and the ability to communicate with a wide range of people.
- Additional technical skills such as a capacity to handle unfamiliar industrial machinery.
- A greater perspective on your career and a deeper commitment to a particular path.

You will also probably gain access to a wider range of opportunities than if you stay on our little islands. Oh, and it can also be fun!

On the other hand, travel can also be a decadent, self-absorbed waste of time. In the words of one anonymous graduate employer: 'If I see one more application from a public schoolboy who's built a bloody schoolhouse in Zambia, saved a coral reef in the Caribbean or climbed Mount Kilimanjaro with his underpants on his head, then I'm going to go mad!'

Therefore, if you do decide to work overseas, make the most of the experience by purposefully developing specific attributes (see Chapter 8).

Grace Lander, recent graduate

As part of my degree in Wildlife Conservation with Zoo Biology, I was given the opportunity to spend a year in industry. I decided to pursue a perfect placement somewhere interesting. I chose three months in Key West, Florida and six months in Anchorage, Alaska (US). By finding something for myself I could really tailor what I got up to. In both Key West and Alaska, I lived onsite at an animal rehabilitation centre, which was a lot of responsibility!

The best part of tailoring something for yourself is choosing what you want to do and how you want to do it. Just make sure you agree terms with your employer in writing so you get as much out of your trip as possible. Due to US visa requirements, I couldn't be paid for my work, so saving up enough to fund the internships was a challenge. The upside is that when you offer yourself up to work for free, people really appreciate the work you're doing, and it looks great on your CV.

The most valuable experience I gained was the time spent learning veterinary procedures and techniques with the team in Alaska. Getting that sort of experience, even as a volunteer in the UK, is next to impossible. It was a fantastic opportunity to get really involved helping with surgical procedures and aftercare. Public educational presentations in Alaska gave me the opportunity to work with live eagles, owls and other birds. Although the public-speaking practice was great, I was also trained in bird handling, a unique skill on my CV! Liaising with the public in both locations and educating large groups about wildlife and nature has given me the confidence to apply for jobs in wildlife education, a passion which was seeded during my placement.

Visas and permission to work

If you travel abroad on some sort of organised placement (whether paid or unpaid), your host will probably arrange all the logistics and visas and so forth. However, if you choose to travel independently, it will almost certainly be down to you.

UK subjects do not need a visa or permission to work in the European Union (EU), The European Economic Area (EEA) or Switzerland (see a full list of these countries in Chapter 5). However, there's still plenty of paperwork. For example, if you stay anywhere in Europe for more than three months, you'll need to apply for an EU resident permit from the relevant authority. This usually involves submitting a whole tranche of documents to the local authorities, such as these:

- Your passport
- Your birth certificate (and marriage certificate if appropriate)
- Proof of accommodation
- Proof you're making contributions to the social security system
- Three photographs
- Your contract of employment.

Outside the EU, every country has its own rules and procedures. Some don't allow visitors of any kind, but others have limited work agreements, and a few have no rules at all. So, it's down to you to research what's allowed and make appropriate provisions. This process can take many months, so start early.

Some good places to start your research are www.gov.uk and the Working Abroad section on www.prospects.ac.uk. Country-specific information can also be found on the relevant government/state department websites or by searching 'working/living in [country]'. You may also want to visit a reputable visa service, such as Trailfinders at www.trailfinders.co.uk/visas.

Some popular visas for young students and graduates include these:

- Australian working holiday visas for young people (18–30 years old) from a range of countries (including the UK and Ireland) to work and travel for a year or two. However, work must not be the main purpose for the visit (note this when you fill out the application). See www.immi.gov.au.
- New Zealand working holiday visas: A similar scheme to Australia's, with a fixed limit of one year and a possible allowance for people up to 35 years of age. See www.immigration.govt.nz.
- Canada: The International Experience Canada programme allows UK citizens to work and travel for up to two years. See www.cic.gc.ca.

Note: These visas have a quota for each year's intake and tend to fill up quickly, so check them out well in advance.

Finding somewhere to live

There are numerous places to lay your head whilst working overseas. If you're taking part in an organised gap-year programme, this should be sorted out for you, but if you've arranged your own opportunity, then you'll probably have to find somewhere to stay, such as your aunt's couch, a tent or a hostel.

Hostels themselves can also be good places to find work, as they are often targeted by local employers who need casual staff. For example, The Cronulla Beach Youth Hostel in Sydney, at www.cronullabeachyha. com, actively markets its ability to help guests find a job and calls itself a 'Backpackers working hostel'.

Good backpacker guides such as those published by Lonely Planet and Rough Guides should let you know where to find work-friendly accommodation. You may also want to talk to fellow travellers on social platforms such as Facebook and just ask around.

In longer-term roles, you'll probably benefit from a more private, salubrious environment. However, unless you're David Beckham, you probably won't be able to afford a £15,000 hotel in town. This isn't so difficult if you're planning on staying for six months or more – just look through the local press and housing agencies for suitable properties. However, it can be tricky if you only want to stay somewhere over summer, because landlords and house-sharers tend to prefer longer commitments. Try the following strategies:

- Ask your future managers and colleagues to sort something out before you leave.
- Try universities as they often rent out student rooms during breaks (especially summer).
- Look on hostel noticeboards, shop windows and websites/social groups where you're working.
- Get there early and hang out with other travellers until something turns up.
- Fire up your social networks and tweet for help.

Remember, if you're planning on living in the EU, EEA or Switzerland for a while, be prepared to fill out lots of paperwork for your residence permit as well as your permission to work.

Volunteering

To their eternal credit, thousands of UK students and graduates head off around the world each year to help less fortunate people and/ or the environment. They take time out after school, make the most of their vacations, leave in the middle of their degrees or just head straight to the airport after graduation, looking for a chance to make a difference. Many volunteers sign up for organised programmes, but others plan their own activities and/or combine a period of volunteering with a paid job and a well-deserved holiday. Find out more below.

Gap-year projects

You can get involved in numerous voluntary programmes across the globe, from looking after kangaroos in Australia (where else?) to building schools in Africa and supporting medical professionals in Japan.

These programmes are usually very expensive, but the money gives you expertise, support and peace of mind. You just have to turn up on time, do what you're told and enjoy.

A sample of some of the more popular gap-year volunteering organisations is provided below:

- Action Aid: www.actionaid.org.uk/adventures – community infrastructure/building projects in Asia and Africa.
- BUNAC: www.bunac.org – volunteering and summer camp programmes in a number of countries (as well as work and internship opportunities).
- Coral Cay Conservation: www.coralcay.org – reef and tropical forest conservation.
- I-to-I: www.i-to-i.com –a wide range of projects from teaching to animal care across the globe.
- Raleigh International: www.raleighinternational.org – community and environmental projects across the globe.

Government/Quasi-government initiatives

If you don't want to work for a private sector organisation but still want the benefits of a tailored voluntary programme, there are also various governmental alternatives. These assignments often provide more extensive experience but less active adventure. Some ideas are listed here:

- The International Citizens Service: www.volunteerics.org – 'a UK government-funded development programme that brings together 18- to 25-year-olds from all backgrounds to fight poverty in overseas and UK communities'.
- Voluntary Services Overseas: www.vso.org.uk – unique roles in developing countries linked to your specific qualifications and experience.

- The European Voluntary Service: www.europa.eu/youth – projects in the EU and beyond for 18- to 30-year-olds. These are unpaid but expenses are covered.
- EU Aid Volunteers: www.ec.europa.eu – online support and active roles for humanitarian organisations around the world.
- British Council European Voluntary Service: www.britishcouncil. org – opportunities for 17- to 30-year-olds of varying length around the globe with expenses and a monthly allowance.

Agencies/Volunteering lists

A number of other organisations also advertise overseas volunteering opportunities such as:

- Anywork Anywhere: www.anyworkanywhere.com – just click on a country to see a list of voluntary projects.
- Go Overseas: www.gooverseas.com – voluntary opportunities mixed with activity breaks, study breaks and internships.
- Go Abroad: www.goabroad.com – similar opportunities with a good search facility.

Creating your own opportunities

A riskier but potentially more empowering alternative is to sort out your own voluntary activities either before you leave or en route. You could try anything – roles linked to your current experience, the career you're chasing or a mini adventure, for example office work in Gibraltar, bookkeeping in Tanzania or fishing in Sri Lanka. However, make sure the activity you want to pursue is permitted under the terms of your visa and, most importantly, it's safe (see Chapter 8). Of course, you'll also have to sort out all the logistics, including travel and accommodation.

There are several ways to identify possible activities:

- Sit back and dream.
- Copy the projects currently being offered by the various gap-year companies.
- Think of accessible roles which will help you develop the career skills you want to develop.

- See what other people are doing on the various traveller websites and social networking groups.
- Identify roles linked to humanitarian/environmental issues which are close to your heart.
- Identify the needs in the countries you want to visit.
- See what opportunities are available in your chosen region.

Once you have some ideas, you need to tee them up. You can either contact people and organisations before you leave or see what turns up on the road. The advantages of organising things before you go are that you can unearth specific opportunities and create a more secure itinerary. Contact people through email or the appropriate social media, tell them a bit about yourself and ask if you can come and help out. Businesses, charities and individuals are often very impressed by such an enterprising approach and will respond positively.

If you decide to look for opportunities as you travel, you'll derive the benefits of spontaneity and seeing what you're in for before making any commitments. You can also ask around and find something that's been highly recommended. However, the activities may well be less structured and relevant to what you really want to do.

Country-specific resources

Most towns, regions and countries across the globe will have organisations and agencies which offer volunteering opportunities, such as the Secrets of Paris Newsletter at www. secretsofparis.com. Here are some ways you can quickly identify what's on offer:

- Look on Twitter and Facebook.
- Enter '[your area]' + 'volunteer' into your search engine.
- Ask at tourist information bureaus.
- Contact the local council and libraries.
- Ask at public bodies such as schools, universities and hospitals.
- Contact local charities.
- Chat to locals over a beer.

Working

Once you've secured a work visa (if one is needed), you can target specific positions. Four of the more common types of roles sought by students and new graduates are explored below:

Casual and seasonal jobs

Many students and new graduates just pick up relatively unskilled roles on their travels, such as labouring and basic telesales. In a similar vein, many people head overseas to take up seasonal positions, usually over the summer months and primarily in roles related to tourism, childcare and sporting pursuits. For example, you could become a festival barman in Denmark, a nanny in France or a ski instructor in Whistler.

With a bit of thought, you can use these roles to develop specific career skills so they look impressive on your CVs and applications. Furthermore, it's a great way to earn some extra pocket money, meet the locals, gain a deeper understanding of new cultures and perhaps even learn a language.

Many of the links in this chapter and Chapter 7 advertise overseas casual/seasonal roles, but some targeted sites include these:

- Season Workers: www.seasonworkers.com – seasonal roles plus childcare, hospitality and much more.
- The Jobs Abroad Bulletin: www.jobsabroadbulletin.co.uk – a wide range of casual positions across the globe and some good advice.
- Universal Jobmatch: www.gov.uk – an extensive European-wide jobs board run by JobCentre Plus in the UK.
- Indeed: www.indeed.co.uk/Seasonal-jobs – temporary posts in a wide range of sectors.
- E4s.co.uk: www.e4s.co.uk – holiday jobs as well as longer-term positions.
- Summer–jobs.co.uk: www.summer-jobs.co.uk – activity-based roles throughout the year.

Once you're on the ground in a foreign country and you want to find work ask at your hostel or hotel; see if the local university has an employment agency; network with other travellers; visit local job agencies; and see if there's a government job centre.

Chapter 7

Internships and placements

Overseas internships are very popular with employers because they clearly show your drive and enterprise. They may also help launch an international career. Overseas internships can be found on many of the links already provided in this chapter and throughout the book, especially those in Chapter 6 such as www.ratemyplacement. co.uk and LinkedIn.com.

International internship programmes A number of organisations offer overseas internships in conjunction with other services such as training, induction, visas and accommodation. The first place to look is Erasmus+ at www.erasmusplus.org.uk – a European Commission programme which aids cross-border cooperation across our continent and all points beyond. Through this initiative, students and recent EU graduates from partner universities (which are listed at www. erasmusprogramme.com) can work abroad for a period from 3 to 12 months and receive a grant to cover expenses.

In the UK, this programme is coordinated by the British Council at www.britishcouncil.org. Positions are promoted on www. erasmusintern.org and can be found on a range of additional sites such as www.eurasmus.com/en. The British Council also coordinates internships around the globe for a range of other organisations.

Other useful sources of posts include:

- AIESEC UK: www.aiesec.co.uk – a youth-led independent organisation providing internships in over 110 countries.
- The Exchange of Students for Technical Experience (IESTE): www. iaeste.org – paid international opportunities (usually over summer) for students of science, engineering and applied arts.

A number of additional opportunities can be found through private agencies such as:

- The Intern Group: www.theinterngroup.com – professional internship programmes in a range of sectors in Hong Kong, Madrid, Melbourne and Colombia (as well as London). Accommodation is provided.
- International Internships: www.international-internships.com – opportunities in Africa, Asia, Europe and both North and South America.

- Go Abroad.com: www.goabroad.com – links to a massive range of opportunities across the globe with a good search facility.
- Glassdoor: www.glassdoor.co.uk – a database of internships across the globe.
- Graduateland: www.graduateland.com – internships at major employers in Europe and beyond.

Country-specific resources Many additional organisations focus on professional roles in particular countries, such as CCI Greenheart at www.cci-exchange.com, which promotes a visa and internships service in the US. You can find jobs in particular countries by:

- Searching for relevant organisations and hashtags on Twitter
- Searching on 'internships in [the particular country]'
- Look up www.prospects.ac.uk/working_abroad.htm
- Using countries' domestic search engines, e.g. www.google.de
- Researching local employers
- Looking at the domestic websites of international organisations
- Surfing student-support web pages at regional universities
- Looking up local professional organisations.

Some useful local links for a host of countries can also be found at www.prospects.ac.uk/working_abroad.htm.

If you're getting an internship as part of a degree programme, make sure your overseas position fits in with your university's guidelines. Remember, you'll also have to fill out a lot of forms if you want to work overseas, such as the EU residence permit, and you may need to sign joint contracts between you, your employer and your university. These are required in many countries such as France, where they're called a 'convention de stage'. Ask for help from your department to see what paperwork may be required.

Some ideas

The table overleaf links some typical overseas opportunities to a range of careers. In the activity at the end of the table, reflect on what you could get up to. You can complete the exercise right here or download it from the companion website at www.palgravecareerskills.com.

How to develop your skills

Opportunity	Some of the skills you could gain
A full-time graduate role as a teacher of English as a foreign language (TEFL) in Japan	• English usage • Teaching • Managing groups of clients • Cultural sensitivity • Flexibility • Creativity
Casual posts as a backpacker in Australia on a year out	• Resourcefulness • The capacity for hard work • Job-specific skills • Organisation • Confidence • Spirit • Personal interaction
An organised gap-year placement	• Organisation • Fundraising • Job-specific skills • Organisation • Confidence • Solving problems • Taking direction
Working over your Easter and Christmas vacations as a ski instructor	• Skiing • Teaching • Client interaction • Organisation • Managing your time • Leadership • Managing resources
Self-assessment: Now, identify an interesting activity for yourself	
What you could do	Skills you could develop (avoid jargon)

How each of these counselling experiences could be used to boost your career in various sectors

Foreign exchange dealer: Learn enough Japanese to work in a financial services company with links between the UK and Japan.

Teach English as a foreign language in the UK: Develop your teaching skills to get onto a UK postgrad TEFL course and teach here.

Sports psychologist: Focus on developing your transferable teaching skills such as listening to client's needs and engaging people.

Speech and language therapist: Look for roles where you'll be helping people out in some way and develop your supporting skills such as identifying problems, listening, advising and training.

Mechanical engineer: Find physical/technical/testing roles where you can learn to solve practical problems under pressure.

Insurance underwriter: Develop your office skills and your ability to organise and manage a heavy technical workload.

Theatre manager: Find some sort of role where you'll be organising entertainment – or put on your own events or shows.

Diplomat: Find opportunities to liaise with local dignitaries and help them out in some way, e.g. organise some sort of charity donation.

IT consultant: Look for a relevant role and/or opportunities to help locals with their IT infrastructure. Reflect on the client interaction skills you gain, as these are key in the industry.

PR: If possible, get involved in any marketing/communications activities either within the firm, through your own social media (e.g. blogging) and/or the wider media.

Civil engineering: Develop high-level client interaction skills so you can promote them to employers in your applications.

Retail banking: Develop the broad range of employability skills required by all employers, especially in relation to customer service.

Your Experience

'Some ideas on how you could make the most of what you do'.

Chapter 7

Steve Rook, author of this guide

From the ages of 18 to 35, I spent most of my time living, travelling, studying and working abroad, largely because I loved it, but also because I had no idea what else to do. Some of the roles I undertook were:

- Bicycle courier in Boston and Sydney
- Dishwasher in Orlando
- Warehouse monkey in Sydney
- Pension seller in Sydney
- Fruit picker in Queensland and Western Australia
- English teacher to refugees on the Thai/Burma border
- Street juggler in New Zealand
- Teacher in New Zealand and Australia
- Recruiter for teachers from Australia to work in the UK

As you can see, I got up to a fair amount, and I wouldn't change it for the world. However, I wish I'd spent more time reflecting on my experiences and working out what I enjoyed most so I could have started my proper professional career rather sooner.

Therefore, I recommend you get out into the big wide world as soon as possible, especially if you're still young and you can sleep on beaches and at bus stops! However, every now and then, pause and reflect on what you're doing and what you're enjoying so you can start to put a plan together for a fulfilling and successful future.

What to do now

People often artificially separate their plans for working overseas from their mainstream career, but this shouldn't be the case in our global village. Therefore, look back at your plans in Chapter 2 to see how you can spice things up a little with a trip or two to the airport.

Managing your journey and staying safe

Contents

On the web

See 'Getting experience without experience' at www.telegraph.co.uk
See 'Making the most of experience' at www.birmingham.ac.uk
See 'Internships and Work Experience' at www.kent.ac.uk/careers
See 'Work experience' at www.careerweb.leeds.ac.uk

Taking control

Of course, experience isn't the end of your journey – it's just the beginning. Therefore, each time you start a new role, you should assess how far you've travelled and immediately plan your next steps. Standing still just isn't an option.

This experience cycle is shown below and outlined in detail throughout the following pages

GG Standing still just isn't an option. JJ

Making the most of your experience

Experience in itself won't really help you in your career, as it's instantly a thing of the past. Therefore, don't just clock in and clock out without giving any thought to what you're actually doing. It's up to you to develop your skills, make contacts and move forward in your journey. In particular, pay attention to the following guidelines.

Impress your boss

Whether you're just starting out or embarking on your sixth internship in a row – it's crucial you strike up a good relationship with your boss. If she likes you

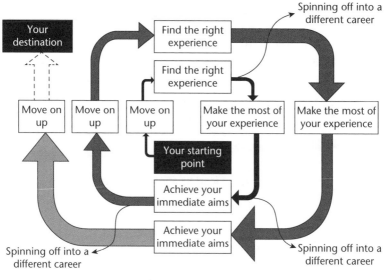

The experience cycle

and respects your work, she will want to keep hold of you and may even give you a promotion. You can command good respect by:

- Turning up on time (five minutes late *is not* 'on time')
- Dressing smartly
- Being clean (invest in an iron and some soap)
- Being reliable (doing what you've said you'd do – on time)
- Being nice and staying positive (you can moan at home).

These personal qualities are generally rated far higher in the world of work than in education, so don't be caught unawares. At first, no one will probably say anything if you transgress, but it will be noted and your prospects instantly restricted. Many of us have learnt this lesson after two or three jobs - save yourself the hassle.

Get on with colleagues and clients

Good relationships with everyone at work are also crucial. Supportive colleagues will watch out for you when you're struggling and help you find further jobs or voluntary positions, both within the organisation and outside. Who knows, the colleagues of today may also be the recruiters of tomorrow. Look for opportunities to build rapport and help out.

Work hard

Needless to say, you'll be respected for putting in the hard graft at work, and sooner or later, this should open up doors. As far as possible, avoid cutting corners and putting in as little effort as possible. This will be noticed, and you will get a reputation for being lazy which will be hard to shake. Instead, go out of your way to perform each task to the best of your ability, and if this means cutting your breaks short or leaving late, so be it.

Perform well

Of course, hard work tends to lead to a job well done, but not necessarily. You also need to be well organised and efficient. These skills can be hard to develop at the start of your working life, but employers will usually be patient if they know you're trying hard and making progress. Consider the following strategies:

- Clarify your role and your specific tasks before jumping in.
- Take responsibility and avoid excuses.
- Be upfront about your level of competence (refrain from putting yourself down or 'bigging' yourself up).
- Ask for help and advice.

- Plan carefully and develop a schedule.
- Assess your progress and keep others in the loop, plus share any difficulties (before it's too late).
- Move heaven and earth to get your work done on time and to a good standard.

Matt Bentley-Walls, Photographer

An example of when I've made the most of my experience occurred 30 years ago. I was as selfish as the next person. I knew I needed to become an assistant fashion photographer in London. I phoned one studio (where I knew most Vogue shoots were conducted) and told them that I had just finished a BTEC in photography and that I would love to come and work for them. I was told that they were currently inviting people to come and work for free for two weeks and someone would be chosen after that. I arrived punctually to find that some had already arrived several days earlier. I set about work knowing full well that I had to make up for lost time.

The single overriding thought I had was that if this were my studio and I were about to take on an assistant, what would I want to see? To me, this was obvious, so I set about ensuring that, for two weeks solidly, I was doing. At no point would the owner of the business walk in and find me chatting or hanging around looking bored. I would be doing something constructive. This could be something as menial as moving lights to a more appropriate place, cleaning a tripod, stripping a camera, painting a backdrop or tidying a desk. It didn't matter as long as I was doing something. I was on a mission. I'd be sociable and approachable but always, always, always doing. When there wasn't anything to do because I'd done everything, I'd invent something.

I also took a strong interest in the business, so if I was interviewed, I could impress them by reeling off 50 things that I thought I could perhaps improve – things I'd taken an interest in and found out about. I also asked a thousand questions, all of which were real and pertinent to the business, some of which might have sounded daft, but I'd ask them anyway to be certain I'd understood. Better, I thought, to find out behind the scenes than in the middle of a front cover shoot for *Vogue* magazine. In this way, I successfully got the one job that was going.

Some might read this and think I behaved in a very manipulative and highly premeditated manner, and perhaps there's some truth in this. However, for me, I'd always maintain that actions speak louder than words.

Chapter 8

Develop your role

Employers look favourably on candidates who've developed themselves within a particular role, as it shows skills and commitment. You can enhance your skills by:

- Focusing on particularly challenging tasks
- Seeking extra duties and/or a promotion
- Talking things through with existing managers.

Also, continually look out for more opportunities. For example, if you want to be a lawyer and you get a part-time job in a law office, you could shadow one of the associates on your day off, or talk your way into a more substantial position. In the following self-assessment, try reflecting on your skills in your current role. You can complete the exercise right here or download it from the companion website at www.palgravecareerskills.com.

Self-assessment: Assessing your career progress

In the table below, list a transferable skill and a technical skill you're trying to develop for your chosen career, and briefly outline how you can improve them in your current role.

Two skills you're trying to develop	How you can develop them in your current role(s)
Example: Client liaison	Asking my boss to let me manage a few of our accounts and generate more business
Your answers: 1. 2.	

Reflecting on your answers: If you can't think of anything, do you need to move on to a new job?

Maximising a placement

After undertaking a placement, you'll probably perform far better in your degree and have a greater chance of getting a good graduate job.[1] However, you shouldn't just take your experience for granted. It will only prove useful if you can take a step back, reflect on how you're doing and improve.

Many placement students are shocked by the sudden changes in lifestyle and the increased levels of responsibility. This is quite natural. However, don't just bottle up your feelings and panic; speak to people and ask for help and advice. For example, reach out to your boss, colleagues, friends on similar programmes and your tutors. Employers understand this is a challenging period and are there to help.

Over the following pages, a number of students and graduates have kindly reflected upon their placement experiences and the challenges they faced. Read through these, and complete the placement planner and review on pages 112 and 113.

Chapter 8

Wilma Wu, international student

Apart from the language barrier, visa and any other international student problems, the real challenge I experienced when I was trying to get work experience was that I did not know what I really wanted to do.

Financial services companies are always very popular among business students, but I just know it is not my thing. I have always known that I wanted to have some work experience, and I know what I am good at. So my solution has been to just keep trying and always keep my eyes on any potential opportunities. I had almost started my master's course when I got my current job as a graduate intern at Leeds University Business School. I enjoy the 'can do' spirit, doing things that I am interested in, developing job skills and knowing I'm progressing. It is really crucial not only in improving my overall employability but also in making me more confident.

Charlotte Hewitt, recent intern

I started on my internship as a trainee ecologist with Avondale Environmental Services a month after initially applying to Step, a graduate recruitment agency. This was a very refreshing experience after I had spent the previous three months job-hunting for graduate schemes and either hearing nothing back or being told I didn't have enough experience. The internship structure of Step placements is ideal, as it provides you with the opportunity to gain experience whilst being paid, but with no obligation to stay beyond the placement if either you or the firm feels it isn't working out. This does, however, mean that a permanent role with the firm is not guaranteed, so I was determined to learn as much as I could in case I needed to job-hunt again after the internship.

This positive attitude to get stuck in really helped me to adapt well to the company and to quickly learn the specialist aspects of working on the railway. I attended courses on arboriculture, protected species and plant identification, which have improved the quality of the site surveys and reports I write. Avondale also encouraged me to participate in volunteering with local stakeholder groups, including the Kent Wildlife Trust. All of these experiences have helped me develop skills which I can build on and take with me as I work towards becoming an ecological consultant.

I am now working full-time for Avondale and I feel fortunate to have undertaken a placement through Step, which gave me an entry into the environmental sector that I can now work upwards from. My advice to anyone struggling to get the job they want is to get out of your comfort zone and to avoid narrowing your search. Take every opportunity for experience you are offered, as you never know when it will become relevant!

Chloe Argon, recent intern

My internship was a constructive and valuable experience as I learnt so much more than ever before. Within my first week, I was allowed to go on a site visit, be involved with huge projects and witness my drawings come to life. This was very rewarding.

Chapter 8

When I first started, I was a little slow because there was so much to learn and I knew I would soon have to pick up the pace and work quickly and reliably. So, I took it upon myself to find ways to improve, such as:

- In my spare time, I researched joinery and various relevant techniques so I could improve my knowledge and skills.
- When I worked on several projects at one time, I prioritised the more urgent requests so I knew I was on schedule (along with my project managers).
- I got out into the workshop to see the construction side of things as well as the management aspect of the projects.
- When it came to liaising with people such as project managers, who were in a different building, I made sure I communicated clearly and took the decision, on my own initiative, to regularly go over to clarify certain issues.
- I set myself goals every week to meet the standards required.

I have now been granted a permanent position with Benchworks, and I can honestly say I am still enjoying my time here and learning something new every day with the supportive team. One piece of advice I can pass on is that, whatever opportunity arises, take it with two hands. It's hard enough for fresh graduates to land themselves a job so, be open to different things. I also believe it's important to have initiative in any workplace so you are able to think for yourself and improve at the same time.

Chapter 8

Alisa Chauhan, placement student

My sandwich placement was based around marketing a healthcare product. A year allowed me to see the preparation to the 'build up' of the product and to form strategies with my manager.

In general, a year is a long time, but well worth it! Sure, the first month may be tough to get settled in; however, afterwards it's just like a second home. A full year also has many perks such as being able to build strong relationships with your colleagues and develop networks throughout your industry (I met a few senior members of the NHS). A year also allows time for personal and professional growth and development. I constantly pushed myself for the better of the company and myself. Being part of a team helped me learn how to judge characters, cooperate and gain trust in colleagues and myself.

The biggest challenges I had were judging characters, working within time limits, understanding the company and what they provide as a whole plus developing an understanding of the healthcare industry. The overall benefits have been that I have reached personal goals, can stand out when I apply for graduate positions and relate theory to practice within my final year (I now have better grades, with a 77 per cent average). Generally, I have become a more mature person and have grown up a lot!

Michael Tefula, recent graduate

I learnt a lot from my internship, but looking back on it now, I wish I had been more vocal about the areas of business that interest me the most. I also wish I had spent more time with senior staff to understand what a 10/20/30-year career looks like.

So my advice is this: don't be afraid to speak up. If there's an area you're interested in, mention it. You only get what you ask for and you'll miss out on lots of opportunities if your employer doesn't know what you want. Also, if senior staff (e.g. partners at consulting and professional services firms) are available, don't be shy about engaging them to learn more about their work. Often times you learn more from someone who's been in the business for decades than from someone who's only been there a couple of years. Be proactive in asking for what you want, don't shy away from speaking with senior staff and you'll find that you learn way more from your internship than if you were to stay quiet and keep to yourself.

Your placement planner and review

Use the templates overleaf to plan what you want to gain from your placement, and reflect on your progress as it draws to an end. You can complete the exercise right here or download it from the companion website at www.palgravecareerskills.com.

Moving on up

Should I stay or should I go?

However much you manage to develop your skills in one role, sooner or later you're probably going to have to move on. You may also be attracted by any number of alternative activities such as going back to university, travelling or setting up your own business. Whatever you do, don't just make rash decisions after a horrible day at the office. Take your time and make strategic choices which will be exciting and fun but also targeted at your ultimate career goal.

Making tracks

There are several things you can do to create a smooth transaction such as:

- Research new paths and make tentative enquiries (although keep these as discrete as possible).
- Apply whilst you're still in post.
- Try new positions out before leaving your old job for good.
- Keep the doors open if you ever want to return.

Also, instead of leaving your current role altogether, you could always try to cut back on your hours and look for additional opportunities in your spare time. In the activity on page 114, look for specific opportunities where you could develop your skills in a new post (this activity matches the one on page 106 where you looked at skills in your existing position). You can compete the exercise tight here or download it from the companion website at www.palgravecareerskills.com.

Outlining your placement goals

Self-assessment: Planning and assessing your placement

At the start of your placement, outline your goals:

- Some technical and transferable skills you hope to gain (be specific and avoid jargon)
- The degree-relevant information you want to pick up
- The challenges you expect and those you actually face.

Before you start your placement	
Two technical skills you hope to gain: 1. 2.	
Two transferable skills you hope to gain: 1. 2.	
Degree-relevant information and knowledge you hope to pick up (for an assignment or otherwise):	
The challenges you expect to face:	The challenges you actually face:

Measuring your achievements near the end of your placement

Self-assessment: How you've carried out your skills

At the end of your placement, outline the goals you've achieved in relation to one of the technical and transferable skills you planned to improve:

- How you've made progress in developing your skills
- The degree-relevant information you've gained
- How you've dealt with your challenges.

At the end of your placement

Three ways you've carried out a technical skill you wanted to develop:

1. The technical skill: ....

2.

3.

Three ways you've carried out a transferable skill you wanted to develop:

1. The transferable skill: ....

2.

3.

Degree-relevant information and knowledge you've picked up:

How you've successfully dealt with your challenges:

Chapter 8

Finding somewhere to develop your skills

Self-assessment: Assessing your career progress

In the table below, list a transferable and a technical skill you're trying to develop for your chosen career, and this time briefly outline how you may be able to improve on them in a *new* role.

Two skills you're trying to develop	Where you could develop them further/new role
1.	
2.	

Reflecting on your answers: Simple question: Will this new experience give you more skills than you can gain in your current role? If so, what's keeping you from moving on? (Good luck!)

A lifelong process

It's worth reaffirming that career planning doesn't end once you get to your immediate destination. New dreams and aspirations will always present themselves however far you get in your life, whether you're 15 or 56. So, don't ever think you should stop reflecting on your skills and proactively managing your path. It's what drives us on as people.

Keep on keeping on

Too many students and graduates give up their dreams after a few slight knockbacks, but you need to persevere because:

- Everything worth having is difficult to get.
- You have much more chance of getting what you want if you're passionate, determined and committed.

However, you should also be resourceful. Don't just keep banging your head against the wall with the same old tactics that haven't worked in the past. In the words of Albert Einstein: 'Insanity is doing the same thing over and over again and expecting different results.'[2] Delve deep into your creativity and enterprise, and find a more effective path. Here are some strategies:

Work your way up

Just get any job or voluntary position, work hard and look for opportunities to get involved in bigger and better things. For example, if you want to run a hotel, get a job as a porter and help out the managers.

Start on another path

Because skills and commitment are so central to success and can be gained in a variety of contexts, career paths regularly intersect. Therefore, if you can't find any way into the career you want, you could start on another tack and cross over when the opportunity presents. For example, if you want to get into management consultancy with a firm that supports the public sector, you could start in NHS management.

Do your research

An in-depth knowledge of your chosen industry will give you the heads-up about important information:

- Where vacancies are likely to occur
- Which organisations are likely to be hiring
- When companies will be taking on new staff
- The skills required
- The key contacts
- The application process.

You can keep abreast of what's happening in particular sectors through media websites and your social networks.

For best results, try to specifically target the exact specialism and sector you want to enter and the relevant organisations. For example, if you want to become a lawyer, you could focus on becoming a solicitor, specialising in family law, at one of the 13 appropriate firms in Scarborough.

Chapter 8

Look for hidden vacancies

Look past the obvious opportunities and find less competitive positions. You can do this through your social networks and sector knowledge. One great tactic is to find advertised vacancies and look for similar roles at other organisations. For example, if Lloyds Bank mounts a popular advertising campaign for interns, see what Barclays and all the other banks are up to. They may have similar vacancies or just be relying on speculative applications. Either way, their unadvertised vacancies are bound to be less competitive.

Adjust your lifestyle

Hard work, enterprise and creativity all feed off a sustainable existence. Therefore, if you're serious about getting your career started, you should also make sure you're in a positive, safe environment. This is tricky in an era of student fees, short-term leases and zero-hour contracts, but you'll reap the benefits if you can find some sort of balance in how you live your life and still maintain a secure roof over your head.

Also, pay attention to a good diet, exercise and healthy living. If you're overextending the welcome from the student union bar and living on deep-fried shish kebabs, then the lights in your upstairs cabinet are bound to start shining with less intensity. You'll be amazed how resourceful you'll become after some home cooking and a few nights on the lemonade.

Become more flexible

When opportunities arise, you need to be in a position to pounce. It's no good saying you can't get to work early in the morning or you don't want to make any further commitments because of your casual job. You've got to make the time. This isn't easy, and it's a fundamentally unfair aspect of modern careers because some students and graduates have much greater flexibility than others. They have cars, financial support, wealthy aunts in London and all the trimmings. However, don't just give up – employers will always notice the sacrifices you've made and welcome your extra drive and commitment.

Better applications

Eighty per cent of CVs and applications are ordinary, poor or downright terrible. Therefore, if you're having trouble getting

experience, this could easily be the reason. Look at the next chapter to
see how you can improve.

Put out feelers

Don't just look for opportunities in your own little bubble. Shout out
your objectives to the treetops. Make sure everyone you know (and
everyone they know) appreciates the sort of opportunities you're after
and helps you out.

Checking out jobs and employers

Unfortunately, a number of recruiters try to take advantage of students
and young workers by misrepresenting what's expected in their
vacancies and the commensurate levels of remuneration. Once you've
been around the block a few times, you'll start to recognise these
unscrupulous employers very quickly because their adverts are usually
vague, over the top and too good to be true, but when you're starting
out, you can easily be taken in. Here are a few tactics you can adopt to
make sure opportunities are for real:

- Check that organisations have a real address (not just a postal box
  or website).
- Verify exactly what's involved.
- Do an Internet search on employers to see what turns up.
- Research through your social contacts.
- If possible, get a contract or at least clear clarification of your pay
  and conditions.
- Discuss the role with your careers service and your student union,
  who may have inside knowledge.

Staying safe

Voluntary organisations and employers have a duty to uphold your
basic human and employment rights, and for the most part, students
and graduates are well treated. However, there are certain things
you can do to make sure your experience is not going to put you in
danger. You can check that:

- You're not being asked to do anything outside your comfort zone.
- You have the freedom to say no and walk away.
- You're getting substantive, useful experience.
- No fees are charged upfront.

Chapter 8

If you're concerned about your safety in any way, contact the careers service at your university, your student union and/or Citizens Advice at www.citizensadvice.org.uk.

Legal and ethical considerations

Of course, you should also make sure that you're not breaking the law. For example, you may have your collar felt if you're leafleting, fly-tipping or using aggressive sales techniques. The last thing you want at this stage of your life is a criminal record ('cautions' go on your criminal record, so avoid them if possible). Therefore, if you're in doubt about the legality of any position, you may want to err on the side of caution and avoid the experience altogether.

Before signing on the dotted line, you should also make sure that particular opportunities match your beliefs and values. For example, if you're thinking of building a school hut in some far-off country for a gap-year organisation, conduct your own due diligence and make sure it's required. (Don't just swallow the company's marketing blurb hook, line and sinker.)

Enjoy

As with life in general, careers are a long excursion into the unknown. Sometimes the sun shines and everything is fine, but on darker days, the going can get tough. However, you should always endeavour to make the best of things. Early career experiences can be especially fraught and difficult, but they can also be great memories as you get older. So, go on – get out there and take on the world with a smile and a thick skin.

What to do now

Get busy, but don't forget to take a step back every week or so to make sure you're still on course for your ultimate objectives.

Applications and interviews

Contents

Useful links

On the web

See 'Graduate jobs – How to impress employers' at www.telegraph.co.uk

See 'Applications and interviews' at www.kent.ac.uk/careers

On YouTube

See Steve Rook in 'How can I prove my skills to employers?', 'How can I perform well in interviews?', and 'How can I stand out from the crowd when applying for jobs?'

On Twitter

#CV
#Interview

Your shop window advertising

Job applications shouldn't be long, boring autobiographies of everything you've ever done in your life. They should be effective marketing tools that clearly show you're right for the job.

You can see what's involved by having a look at supermarket posters on the high street. These short, enticing adverts are simply designed to draw shoppers in. This is what you're applications should do. Only, instead of crisps, holidays and toilet rolls, you need to sell your skills, commitment and knowledge. You can find out more about applications in *The Graduate Career Guidebook* (Rook, 2013).

> 66 Job applications shouldn't be long, boring autobiographies of everything you've ever done in your life. 99

How to succeed

Recruitment isn't a random beauty contest (thank God) where you have to vainly and vaguely argue why you're such a good catch, but a specific, targeted process of proving you're the best candidate because of your relevant skills, commitment and knowledge. This is achieved by carefully identifying the attributes required and proving you have them, as outlined below.

Identify what's required

The first step to giving people what they want is asking them what it is! More often than not, applicants forget this step in the application process and spend hours trying to imagine what they need to promote about themselves. What a waste of time – just *ask*. In fact, with most applications, you don't even have to look too deeply to find out what attributes are required; they're listed right there in the job adverts and personal specifications.

Skills and commitment are typically held in greater esteem by employers than knowledge because:

- Information is freely available in today's world.
- If you know what you're doing and you really want the job, you'll soon pick up everything you need to know.

Therefore, before putting pen to paper in your applications, take some time to pick out what's required. You can practise forensically assessing job requirements in the following exercise (the answers are provided below so cover them up before you look). You can complete the exercise right here or download it from the companion website at www.palgravecareerskills.com.

Mark Peterson, OSIsoft EMEA

The keys to getting a graduate job are the commitment to research the organisation, the initiative to differentiate yourself and the ability to create a good first impression.

Self-assessment: Identifying specific job criteria in job descriptions and personal specifications

Identify the experience, skills, commitment and knowledge required in the following teaching position.

Job description and personal specification for a maths tutor

We can give you the opportunity to work with well-motivated children in an outstanding school which is innovative and forward-thinking. You will also gain the full support of a professional team of staff, opportunities for professional development and an attractive location in semi-rural Cheshire.

Are You Someone Who:

- Has six months' relevant experience?
- Is an inspirational and passionate teacher of maths?
- Has a desire to further improve what we offer?
- Wants to make a real difference to the lives of young people?
- Is able to teach the full range of age and ability across KS3, GCSE and A Level?

Reflecting on your answers: If you just picked out the obvious criteria listed in the bullet points, you need to get used to looking deeper. Practise with some real-life vacancies for the roles you're seeking.

The answers:

- **Experience:** six months' relevant experience.
- **Skills:** outstanding teaching, motivating children and support colleagues plus being an inspirational and passionate teacher with the capacity to teach the full range of ages and ability.
- **Commitment:** being forward thinking, committed to professional development, happy to live in a semi-rural community, have a desire to improve what the school offers and make a real difference to young people's lives, committed to professional development (again) and high standards.
- **Knowledge:** maths curriculum across KS3, GCSE and A Level.

There are also numerous additional ways to research the attributes required by specific employers, like these:

- Just picking up the phone and having a chat
- Looking on the Twittersphere® and LinkedIn
- Studying their websites
- Looking up on forums such as those on www.thestudentroom. co.uk.

Prove your relevant attributes

Once you've identified the unique selection criteria for particular positions, you can set about proving your employability, i.e. that you have what's required.

Your qualifications Briefly outline what they are and why they're relevant. As time goes by, your school qualifications will become less important.

Your experience This is a peculiar assessment criterion which is increasingly stipulated for even the most basic roles. It is of questionable use, however, because the fact that you've done a job doesn't necessarily mean you're any good! Off the record, many employers admit that it is just a blunt expediency to narrow down the number of applications whilst maintaining high standards.

The good news is that this requirement is usually quite vague. Therefore, in most applications, you usually have the opportunity to draw from any roles in your life as long as you can demonstrate they fit. For example, the personal specification above simply stipulates 'six months' relevant experience'. You could prove this by amalgamating your time spent on any number of activities such as helping out at a local school, teaching your neighbour's children as well as any formal roles you've undertaken.

Your skills It's harder to prove your skills than it sounds, but it gets easier with practice. This is because it's not sufficient to just list various examples. You also need to outline your specific strengths. You can do this by demonstrating:

- *How* you perform the skill to a high level
- *When* you have performed the skill well (through a specific example).

For instance, you could describe your organisation and cooking skills as follows:

Organisation

How you demonstrate the skill	A specific example of **when** you demonstrated it
Setting targets, planning carefully and regularly reviewing progress.	Funding my gap year to Chile.

Cooking

How you demonstrate the skill	A specific example of **when** you demonstrated it
Fast at picking up new techniques, good attention to detail and ability to quickly learn new recipes.	Last summer, during a particularly busy evening at 'The Rose and Crown'.

Now you've seen how it's done, try it for yourself. In the following exercise, describe how and when you have performed two of the skills required in your chosen career. You can complete the exercise right here or download it from the companion website at www. palgravecareerskills.com.

Chapter 9

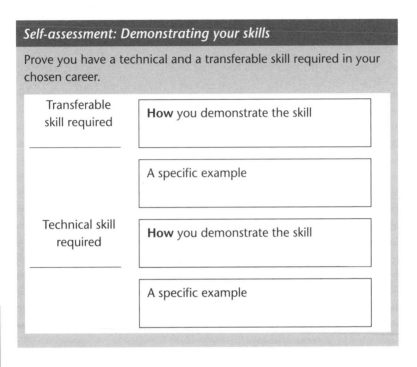

Your commitment Of course, skills alone don't prove your potential; you also need to prove you have the necessary commitment, that is the desire and drive to succeed. You can do this as follows:

1. Research the position: Nothing shows more interest in a vacancy than a real understanding of the role, the sector and the specific job.
2. Demonstrate why you've applied: Outline what attracts you to that particular industry, organisation and role. This demonstrates that you've done your research and reflected on what you have to offer.
3. Show how you've targeted that specific role: Demonstrate how you've actively gone about pursuing that exact position and how your experience has confirmed that you have chosen the right path.

Proving your knowledge Employers often test you on job-specific concepts and processes, so read up on these and lightly sprinkle some technical terms in your applications. However, stick to what you know, as you'll probably be asked about what you've written at your interview.

Your CV

The traditional vehicle for selling yourself to employers is your CV. These documents are now used less widely, but they still feature strongly at the start of your experience journey.

The need to target

Most people construct their CVs by listing everything they've ever done in their lives in the simple hope that employers will quickly infer they're right for the job. They won't. They don't have the time! To impress recruiters, you need to target your document at the specific skills required. **Therefore, there's no such thing as 'my CV', only your CV for each particular role**. You can target your CVs as follows:

1. Identify the specific skills required.
2. Pinpoint exactly when in your life you have best demonstrated them.
3. Briefly list your key experiences and achievements and clearly outline in detail *how* they prove the specific skills required.
4. Once you've proven each skill, cross it off your list, as there's no need to prove the same skill over and over again.

Spelling and grammar

Most CVs find the bin very quickly because they have numerous spelling and grammatical errors. This is inexcusable. Academics often overlook these indiscretions when marking assignments, so students can get lazy, but employers won't be as forgiving. Therefore, don't just send off your CV as soon as it's finished; take a break and review it when your mind is fresh, and get someone else to look over it, just to make sure it's okay.

Rules and conventions

- Use two pages unless you've been otherwise advised or you're going for a financial role in The City (when one will usually do).
- Make sure your headings are clear and well highlighted.
- Put key information at the top of each page.
- List the most recent events first.
- Use your name as the main heading, and don't bother writing 'Curriculum Vitae'.
- Make sure your key attributes stand out at first glance.
- Make sure the dates are easy to see and there are no gaps.

Chapter 9

What to include

Simple – just put in what you think will help you get the job, and avoid everything else. For example, if you got poor A-level grades, you could consider leaving them out. Most CVs will have the sections listed below. Look at the example CVs in the following pages to see how they look in practice.

- A summary/personal profile
- Personal details
- Education

- Experience
- Interests
- References

Other popular headings include 'Positions of Responsibility', 'Personal Attributes' and 'Achievements', but you should amend yours in any way to promote your unique attributes.

Should you push the truth?

When you're chatting someone up in a pub, you don't tell him or her about your smelly socks and awful taste in music (hopefully). You present yourself in the best possible light. This is what you need to do in your CVs. In other words, avoid anything that may hold you back (such as poor grades or differences of opinion at work), and stress your experiences which best promote what you have to offer. For example, in CV1 following, the candidate outlines his experience at a firm of accountants and the skills he demonstrated. However, he doesn't let on that his dad owns the firm and he only popped in periodically. So, push your positive experiences, even if they were only a minor part of a particular role, but don't lie.

The two main CV formats

Employers are accustomed to seeing two main types of CV: 'chronological/traditional' and 'skills-based'. Unfortunately, graduates often assume that chronological CVs should focus on experience, whereas skills-based CVs should emphasise your key attributes. This is not true. Traditional and skills-based CVs should both highlight your skills; they are just structured differently.

Skills-based CVs Skills-based CVs, such as CV1 and CV2 overleaf, outline your relevant education, employment experience and interests in one section, and collate your skills together under an additional heading. The skills section should therefore have examples from every walk of your life, especially your time at work.

Chronological/Traditional CVs These documents directly link your education, work experience and interests to your relevant skills. See CV3 below.

The skills-based CV is generally recommended at the start of your career journey, when you don't have a great deal of relevant experience. The chronological format can work more effectively when you have a more significant work record.

How long should it take to write your CV?

Success in recruitment is down to the quality of your applications, not the quantity. Unfortunately, however, employers quickly dismiss the majority of CVs because they're untargeted and full of spelling/grammatical errors. Therefore, you need to carefully target your CVs at the unique skills required in each new vacancy and use impeccable English. This takes time – about 10 to 20 hours per document. Sure, you can just adapt old CVs in half an hour, but you probably won't get the job, so what's the point?

Many busy students will baulk at this time commitment when they're sending off lots of applications – here, there and everywhere – but it actually saves time. This is because the targeted approach allows you to send off far fewer submissions. In other words, if you spend 20 or so hours on one excellent, targeted CV, it is far more likely to draw dividends than 20 that are vague, generic and poor (which will take the same amount of time).

Example CVs

Three example CVs are presented over the next six pages for a customer-facing role supporting small local businesses. The key requisites for the job are listed first. CV1 is from a student just starting out on his career; CV2 is from a student with some experience; and CV3 is from a graduate with a more relevant degree and a significant work record.

The description for the following CVs lists these job requirements:

- **Skills** in customer service, written and spoken communication, teamwork, liaison with colleagues, analysis, IT, management and commercial awareness.
- **Personal qualities** of adaptability, initiative, enthusiasm, creativity and a commitment to hard work.

Example CV1 – a skills-based CV (sent in early 2016 from a student just starting out on the experience journey):

Experience is split into two sections to highlight the more relevant work history.	Most students and new graduates put education at the head of their CVs, as their degrees are their main selling points.	Use reverse chronological order (put your most recent experiences first).

Include your most relevant social network details (usually LinkedIn).

David Davies

D.davies@email.com
07565 678 6551
www.uk.linkedin/myname
20 Tee Park, Plymouth, PL4 2PY

If your degree isn't obviously relevant, outline what you've done that is.

Education

2015–present   **South Plymouth University, BA English**
Written and spoken communication in a range of modern contexts.

2009–2015   **Childs Hill School, Plymouth**
A Levels: English B, French B, History B
9 GCSEs including A grades at English and maths

Provide more detail for your degree than your school qualifications, as they are now old hat.

Work experience
Summer 2015   **John's Toys, Kew, Salesperson/Supervisor**
• Ensuring customer service satisfaction in a busy inner-city store.
• Supporting customers with complaints.

School holidays from 2012–2015   **JTE Accountants, London, various roles**
• General office duties such as designing office templates and directing new customers.
• Marketing the firm via Twitter and writing the company's blog.

This candidate really makes the most of his experience because he only actually went to work at his dad's firm once or twice

Additional experience 10/2015 – present   **University Business Society**
Visiting local businesses to find out more about their industries.

2013–2015   **School Entrepreneurship Society**
Learning fundamental business concepts, marketing and digital bookkeeping.

Interests
• Making toys for my local school and selling them online (with a profit, so far this year, of £346).

Make the most of all your experience (paid or unpaid)

Chapter 9

Skills are taken directly from the job advert. Don't be afraid to use the same words and make sure they stand out.

Bullet points can make the skills easier to scan.

Using the first person ('I') is increasingly okay, and it gives a more personal touch, but avoid it in CVs for more traditional employers.

Skills Profile

Customer service/Commercial awareness/Hard work
At John's Toys, I was awarded a sales bonus because I diligently:
- Ensured that product queries led to sales.
- Focused on continually improving my sales techniques to achieve ambitious targets.

Clearly link your previous experience to the specific skills required in each role.

Written and spoken communication
- At JTE Accountants, I was universally praised for my excellent promotional tweets and interesting Facebook articles.
- I speak clearly and carefully adjust my message to the situation and audience. For example, I am enthusiastic with customers and calm with colleagues but always happy to listen.

Teamwork/Liaison with colleagues/Enthusiasm
At John's Toys, I motivated my team to achieve record sales by:
- Quickly taking personal responsibility for my own tasks.
- Supporting others and making sure everyone felt positive.

IT
I am happy to use a wide range of software, as demonstrated through my analysis of sales figures at John's Toys and in my eBay buying and selling business.

Management
I lead by listening, encouraging others and providing support. For example, at John's Toys I supervised colleagues in a project to offload old lines, helping us sell more units than any of our other stores.

Adaptability/Initiative/Creativity
I derive great fulfilment from looking at business problems and finding new solutions. For example, I recently turned around disappointing sales for the toys I sell on eBay by promoting them as part of a general educational programme linked to the National Curriculum.

References
Academic: Dr B. E. Learned, personal tutor, S. Plymouth University, Plymouth PL1 4TY, 01752 645 3456, learned@splymouth.ac.uk.
Professional: Mr M. Manager, Store Manager, John's Toys London, WC1 2GE, 0107 554 6778, m.manager@johnstoys.co.uk.

Always include your referees' details unless you have a good reason not to, such as you don't want them to know you're going for another job. In that case, you can just state 'References on request'.

Chapter 9

Example CV2 – a skills-based CV (sent in early 2016 from a student with some good experience):

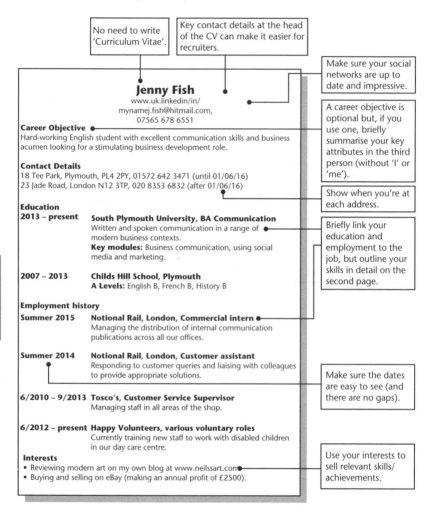

No need to write 'Curriculum Vitae'.

Key contact details at the head of the CV can make it easier for recruiters.

Make sure your social networks are up to date and impressive.

A career objective is optional but, if you use one, briefly summarise your key attributes in the third person (without 'I' or 'me').

Show when you're at each address.

Briefly link your education and employment to the job, but outline your skills in detail on the second page.

Make sure the dates are easy to see (and there are no gaps).

Use your interests to sell relevant skills/ achievements.

Jenny Fish
www.uk.linkedin/in/
mynamej.fish@hitmail.com,
07565 678 6551

Career Objective
Hard-working English student with excellent communication skills and business acumen looking for a stimulating business development role.

Contact Details
18 Tee Park, Plymouth, PL4 2PY, 01572 642 3471 (until 01/06/16)
23 Jade Road, London N12 3TP, 020 8353 6832 (after 01/06/16)

Education
2013 – present   **South Plymouth University, BA Communication**
Written and spoken communication in a range of modern business contexts.
Key modules: Business communication, using social media and marketing.

2007 – 2013   **Childs Hill School, Plymouth**
A Levels: English B, French B, History B

Employment history
Summer 2015   **Notional Rail, London, Commercial intern**
Managing the distribution of internal communication publications across all our offices.

Summer 2014   **Notional Rail, London, Customer assistant**
Responding to customer queries and liaising with colleagues to provide appropriate solutions.

6/2010 – 9/2013   **Tosco's, Customer Service Supervisor**
Managing staff in all areas of the shop.

6/2012 – present   **Happy Volunteers, various voluntary roles**
Currently training new staff to work with disabled children in our day care centre.

Interests
• Reviewing modern art on my own blog at www.neilssart.com
• Buying and selling on eBay (making an annual profit of £2500).

Specific experiences should be taken from every walk of life, but primarily from your employment experience.

The list of skills should be copied directly from the job description, but some can be amalgamated so there are only seven or eight titles in total.

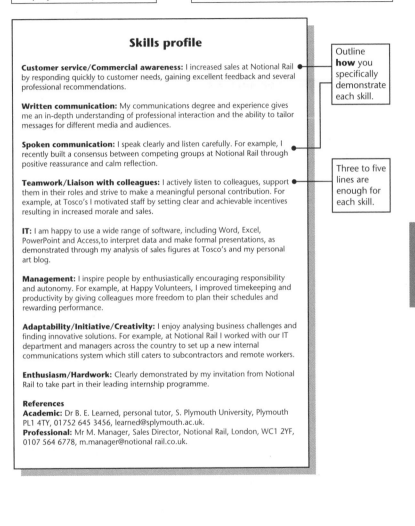

Skills profile

Customer service/Commercial awareness: I increased sales at Notional Rail by responding quickly to customer needs, gaining excellent feedback and several professional recommendations.

Written communication: My communications degree and experience gives me an in-depth understanding of professional interaction and the ability to tailor messages for different media and audiences.

Spoken communication: I speak clearly and listen carefully. For example, I recently built a consensus between competing groups at Notional Rail through positive reassurance and calm reflection.

Teamwork/Liaison with colleagues: I actively listen to colleagues, support them in their roles and strive to make a meaningful personal contribution. For example, at Tosco's I motivated staff by setting clear and achievable incentives resulting in increased morale and sales.

IT: I am happy to use a wide range of software, including Word, Excel, PowerPoint and Access, to interpret data and make formal presentations, as demonstrated through my analysis of sales figures at Tosco's and my personal art blog.

Management: I inspire people by enthusiastically encouraging responsibility and autonomy. For example, at Happy Volunteers, I improved timekeeping and productivity by giving colleagues more freedom to plan their schedules and rewarding performance.

Adaptability/Initiative/Creativity: I enjoy analysing business challenges and finding innovative solutions. For example, at Notional Rail I worked with our IT department and managers across the country to set up a new internal communications system which still caters to subcontractors and remote workers.

Enthusiasm/Hardwork: Clearly demonstrated by my invitation from Notional Rail to take part in their leading internship programme.

References
Academic: Dr B. E. Learned, personal tutor, S. Plymouth University, Plymouth PL1 4TY, 01752 645 3456, learned@splymouth.ac.uk.
Professional: Mr M. Manager, Sales Director, Notional Rail, London, WC1 2YF, 0107 564 6778, m.manager@notional rail.co.uk.

Outline **how** you specifically demonstrate each skill.

Three to five lines are enough for each skill.

Example CV3 – a chronological CV (sent in early 2016 from a graduate with excellent experience):

> Try to get your best experiences on the top page.

> You only need to prove each skill once.

Yupeng Chan

y.chan@hitmail.com, 07545 678 6551,
www.uk.linkedin/in/myname
23 Jade Road, London N12 3TP, 020 8353 6832

Summary ●────
Well-qualified business graduate with two years' business experience Including a prize-winning internship advising local businesses.

> Use any headings you think will help such as 'Summary'.

Education
2012–2015 South Plymouth University, BA Business
Relevant modules:

- Business accounting
- Microeconomics
- Macroeconomics
- Enterprise ●────
- International business
- Marketing

> If your degree is relevant, outline what you've done.

Dissertation: Supporting business in modern industry ●────

Skills gained: ●────
Commercial awareness – an in depth appreciation of the factors affecting modern business and the need to continually focus on sales and customer satisfaction.
Written communication – writing for business and adjusting the message to the audience/medium.

> Systematically link each of your experiences to one or two of the skills required.

2006–2012 Childs Hill School, Plymouth
A Levels: English A, Maths A, Economics B

Relevant experience
Summer 2015   **Business Local Link, London, Sales intern**

- Advising local business on using social media, website development and digital marketing. ●────
- Setting up a new Facebook page for local small business.
- Managing sales for three key accounts.

> Outline your relevant duties and the skills you gained/demonstrated.

Skills gained
Customer service – supporting a diverse range of clients with all issues related to business start-up and upselling our business development products. ●────
IT – confident with all Office products, accounting software and social networks.

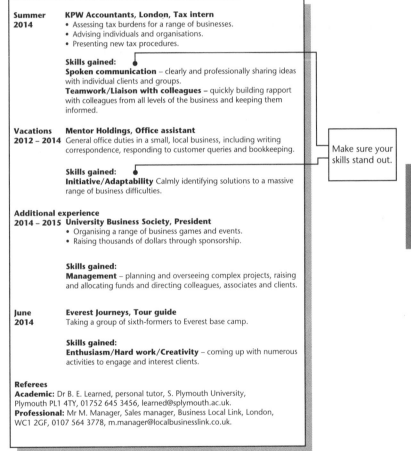

Summer 2014   **KPW Accountants, London, Tax intern**
- Assessing tax burdens for a range of businesses.
- Advising individuals and organisations.
- Presenting new tax procedures.

Skills gained:
Spoken communication – clearly and professionally sharing ideas with individual clients and groups.
Teamwork/Liaison with colleagues – quickly building rapport with colleagues from all levels of the business and keeping them informed.

Vacations 2012 – 2014   **Mentor Holdings, Office assistant**
General office duties in a small, local business, including writing correspondence, responding to customer queries and bookkeeping.

Skills gained:
Initiative/Adaptability Calmly identifying solutions to a massive range of business difficulties.

Additional experience
2014 – 2015   **University Business Society, President**
- Organising a range of business games and events.
- Raising thousands of dollars through sponsorship.

Skills gained:
Management – planning and overseeing complex projects, raising and allocating funds and directing colleagues, associates and clients.

June 2014   **Everest Journeys, Tour guide**
Taking a group of sixth-formers to Everest base camp.

Skills gained:
Enthusiasm/Hard work/Creativity – coming up with numerous activities to engage and interest clients.

Referees
Academic: Dr B. E. Learned, personal tutor, S. Plymouth University, Plymouth PL1 4TY, 01752 645 3456, learned@splymouth.ac.uk.
Professional: Mr M. Manager, Sales manager, Business Local Link, London, WC1 2GF, 0107 564 3778, m.manager@localbusinesslink.co.uk.

Make sure your skills stand out.

Chapter 9

Application forms

Application forms have increasingly usurped CVs, especially since the advent of the Internet. This is because they're easier for employers to administer and can be used to test specific skills. However, the majority of forms received by recruiters are still unfocused and littered with mistakes. Therefore, with just a little bit of work, you can quickly jump the queue.

Outlining your experience

In most forms there's a section for you to outline your previous jobs. Don't worry if you haven't done much, as you can also usually draw from your more formal unpaid experiences. However, don't just list your responsibilities in a vacuum. Look at the requirements of the job you're going for, and focus on the activities that relate (even if they were only a minor part of the role).

The tricky questions

The skills questions on application forms are universally feared, but they are simply an attempt on the part of recruiters to force you to prove *how* you demonstrate their required attributes and provide *specific examples*. Whether the questions are short and punchy or long and convoluted, you can structure your answers in line with the following STAR technique by outlining:

S – a focused **situation** where you used the specific skill.
T – your **task**, i.e. what you did.
A – your **actions**, i.e. three ways you performed the skill well.
R – the **result**, i.e. what you learned or achieved.

Situation – 10%
Task – 10%
Actions – 70%
Result – 10%

The STAR technique for answering questions on application forms.

As the STAR mnemonic suggests, if you are given a tight word limit, you can barely allow a single sentence for the situation, task and result in your answers because employers primarily want to see how you demonstrate the particular skills they need. A good answer is shown below for a typical question on teamwork, but you should note, even if the question is much simpler, such as 'Tell us about your teamwork skills', then the answer should still, pretty much, follow the same format. Always provide a specific example, *whether or not one is requested*, and stick to the word or character limit.

An example skills-based question and answer for an application form:

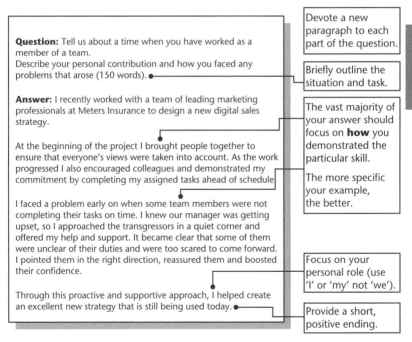

Question: Tell us about a time when you have worked as a member of a team.
Describe your personal contribution and how you faced any problems that arose (150 words).

Answer: I recently worked with a team of leading marketing professionals at Meters Insurance to design a new digital sales strategy.

At the beginning of the project I brought people together to ensure that everyone's views were taken into account. As the work progressed I also encouraged colleagues and demonstrated my commitment by completing my assigned tasks ahead of schedule

I faced a problem early on when some team members were not completing their tasks on time. I knew our manager was getting upset, so I approached the transgressors in a quiet corner and offered my help and support. It became clear that some of them were unclear of their duties and were too scared to come forward. I pointed them in the right direction, reassured them and boosted their confidence.

Through this proactive and supportive approach, I helped create an excellent new strategy that is still being used today.

Devote a new paragraph to each part of the question.

Briefly outline the situation and task.

The vast majority of your answer should focus on **how** you demonstrated the particular skill.

The more specific your example, the better.

Focus on your personal role (use 'I' or 'my' not 'we').

Provide a short, positive ending.

Chapter 9

Now you've learned the ropes, try proving your communication skills in the following exercise. You can complete the exercise right here or download it from the companion website at www.palgravecareerskills.com.

Self-assessment: Answering a skills-based application form question

Use the STAR technique to answer the following question

Question: What are your communication skills?

Answer:

Reflecting on your answers:
Did you follow the STAR technique?
Did you use a *specific example* and outline *how* you performed your communication skills in three specific ways?
Did you use positive words, and is your spelling/grammar up to scratch? (Ask someone else to check.)

Personal statements

Some application forms invite you to complete a general statement outlining why you're attracted to the role and/or what makes you suitable. Complete them as shown in the following template:

How to write a personal statement:

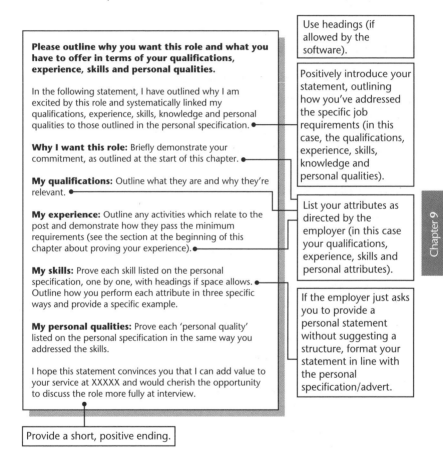

Please outline why you want this role and what you have to offer in terms of your qualifications, experience, skills and personal qualities.

In the following statement, I have outlined why I am excited by this role and systematically linked my qualifications, experience, skills, knowledge and personal qualities to those outlined in the personal specification.

Why I want this role: Briefly demonstrate your commitment, as outlined at the start of this chapter.

My qualifications: Outline what they are and why they're relevant.

My experience: Outline any activities which relate to the post and demonstrate how they pass the minimum requirements (see the section at the beginning of this chapter about proving your experience).

My skills: Prove each skill listed on the personal specification, one by one, with headings if space allows. Outline how you perform each attribute in three specific ways and provide a specific example.

My personal qualities: Prove each 'personal quality' listed on the personal specification in the same way you addressed the skills.

I hope this statement convinces you that I can add value to your service at XXXXX and would cherish the opportunity to discuss the role more fully at interview.

Use headings (if allowed by the software).

Positively introduce your statement, outlining how you've addressed the specific job requirements (in this case, the qualifications, experience, skills, knowledge and personal qualities).

List your attributes as directed by the employer (in this case your qualifications, experience, skills and personal attributes).

If the employer just asks you to provide a personal statement without suggesting a structure, format your statement in line with the personal specification/advert.

Provide a short, positive ending.

Online applications

Many graduate employers now expect you to apply online – here are some guidelines:

- Familiarise yourself with the organisation's system.
- Don't rush the answers.

- Write your answers in Word (or any other reliable word processing programme) and save them regularly; then transfer them over to the form when you've finished.
- Edit your answers to get rid of any gremlins.
- Print out your answers to check them.
- Save your work and return to it later so you can reflect on what you've written.
- Don't leave the form to the last minute, as computers and networks regularly crash.

If you have any questions about what's expected or you have particular issues, contact the employer directly for advice before getting started. For example, ask what to do if you don't have the grades required but have mitigating circumstances, or if you have a disability requiring an alternative format.

Speculative applications

Once you've made a few good career contacts, you can proactively approach them for experience. For example, you could help your dad at his shop, your first cousin's friend's sister at her acting studio or a LinkedIn connection at his office. As a general rule, small, medium and new-start organisations tend to be more flexible and open to this approach. Don't be too proud to accept any casual position at the outset because, once you've got your foot in the door, you can hopefully talk your way into better roles. The traditional route into this sort of experience is through a targeted CV and cover letter, but social media is quickly becoming the tool to use. Whether or not you expect to be paid, it's probably not worth mentioning payment in your first interaction. Use the following technique:

Step 1 Identifying positions Identify some sectors and organisations where you'd like to get involved. These may be linked to the specific career you're targeting, but not necessarily, as you can develop skills in any role. For example, you may want to be a doctor, but a good starting point might be in a social care setting such as driving old people to the shops or helping special needs children at school. You can research specific sectors at www.prospects.ac.uk and www.direct. gov.uk/NationalCareersService. Find specific employers on LinkedIn and Google.

Don't just focus on the main firms that advertise student and graduate opportunities. Proactively look for their less-obvious competitors who may rely on a more informal approach.

Step 2 Research the specific organisations you're targeting to identify their key interests and challenges. Look through:

- The firms' own websites
- Their social sites
- National news sites such as The Guardian (www.theguardian.com) and the BBC (www.bbc.co.uk).

Step 3 Get in touch (preferably through your existing contacts), and suggest how you can help. Don't just send your CV to an unnamed post office box or the firm's general email address – you'll probably never hear back. You need to get in touch with a specific person at each organisation.

Cover letters

You should always send a cover letter with your CVs and application forms unless you've been expressly told not to or it's not possible with an online application.

What to include

Your cover letter should include your name and address, the name and address of the person you are addressing (always send it to a named person) and a brief and positive outline of what attracts you about the post and your key attributes (which you have outlined on your CV or application form). Just like your CV, your cover letter should be targeted at the specific role for which you are applying. If you are sending your CV as an attachment to an email, send the cover letter as another attachment.

Suggested structure

Use one side of A4 and highlight relevant skills and experiences using the structure shown below.

How to format a cover letter:

Chapter 9

Your full name and address

Name of person to be contacted
Address of organisation
Date

Dear (name of person),

APPLICATION FOR THE POSITION OF ... (Ref. no.)

Paragraph 1: Introduce yourself formally and positively and outline how you heard about the opportunity (avoid informal statements such as 'Hello, my name is Joe Smith, and I am writing this letter ...').

Paragraph 2: Explain why you are interested in the opportunity and the organisation. Demonstrate that you have researched the opportunity and have thought deeply about why you're attracted.

Paragraphs 3–4: Outline why you are suitable. Draw the reader's attention to your key skills and experiences that are outlined in full on your CV.

Paragraph 5: Include a polite and positive ending.

Yours sincerely,
(If you have addressed the letter to 'Dear Sir/Madam', close your letter with the statement 'Yours faithfully'.)

Your signature
Your name

Hannah Moger, Special Project Manager, University of Leicester

To be successful in their applications, students should clearly articulate their motivation for each role and organisation, and demonstrate that they have the skills and capability to be effective and that they have achieved more than just a degree whilst at university, by getting involved in extracurricular opportunities such as student societies, work experience and volunteering.

Psychometric tests

Verbal and numeric reasoning tests are increasingly used by recruiters to assess candidates for internship opportunities. Contrary to popular opinion, they aren't designed to test your basic numeracy and written English skills, but your capacity to synthesise information in numeric and written form and make accurate inferences. It is widely held that this reasoning ability is largely innate and immutable in each of us and that these tests are therefore a good measure of inherent ability. The most common tests are outlined below.

Verbal reasoning tests

Verbal reasoning tests appraise your vocabulary, comprehension and ability to identify relationships. They typically comprise several passages of text linked to a handful of statements. You are usually expected to identify whether these statements are 'true', 'false' or you 'cannot say', based solely on what's been written in the text. In other words, you're not simply being asked whether the statements are true, false or you cannot say, but whether or not the text confirms this. For example, a question on the following passage could ask if internal combustion engines are used to power most cars. The correct answer would be 'Cannot say' because the text does not confirm or deny this fact (even though it is, in fact, true).

> In internal combustion engines, the combustion of a fuel (normally a fossil fuel) occurs with an oxidizer (usually air) in a combustion chamber that is an integral part of the working fluid flow circuit. The first commercially successful internal combustion engine was created by Étienne Lenoir.

Have a go yourself Four typical questions are shown overleaf based on a short text on Judaism – see how you get on. Answers are provided on page 143. You can complete the exercise right here or download it from the companion website at www. palgravecareerskills.com.

Self-assessment: A short verbal reasoning test

Read the following text and answer the following questions

Judaism is the religion, philosophy and way of life of the Jewish people. It is a monotheistic religion originating in the Tanakh and explored in later texts such as the Talmud. According to Rabbinic Judaism, God revealed his laws and commandments on Mount Sinai to Moses in the Written and Oral Torah. Jews are an ethnoreligious group which includes people born as Jews who convert to Judaism. Judaism has been followed continually for over 3000 years. It is one of the oldest monotheistic religions and the oldest to survive into the present day. Judaism strongly influenced later Abrahamic religions, including Christianity and Islam, and has therefore directly or indirectly influenced secular Western ethics and civil law.

1. Judaism is a monotheistic religion because it is so old.

    a. The passage confirms this statement is true.
    b. The passage confirms this statement is false.
    c. The passage is inconclusive.

2. There have never been older monotheistic religions than Judaism.

    a. The passage confirms this statement is true.
    b. The passage confirms it is false.
    c. The passage is inconclusive.

3. Abrahamic religions are strongly influenced by Judaism.

    a. The passage confirms this statement is true.
    b. The passage confirms it is false.
    c. The passage is inconclusive.

4. Rabbinic Judaism holds that God revealed his laws and commandments to Moses in the form of the Written Torah.

    a. The passage confirms this statement is true.
    b. The passage confirms it is false.
    c. The passage is inconclusive.

Chapter 9

The answers:

1. c – The text does not go into why Judaism is monotheistic.

2. c – Even though Judaism is the oldest monotheistic religion that exists today, older monotheistic religions may have existed in the past.

3. a – This is clearly stated in the text.

4. a – This is clearly stated in the text. You may have been put off by the fact that the text also states that God revealed his laws in Oral Torah, but this has no impact on the answer.

Numeric reasoning tests

Numeric tests typically examine your ability to work with numbers and graphs. You're usually allowed a calculator.

Have a go yourself Try answering the following questions – the answers are provided below. You can complete the exercise right here or download it from the companion website at www.palgravecareerskills.com.

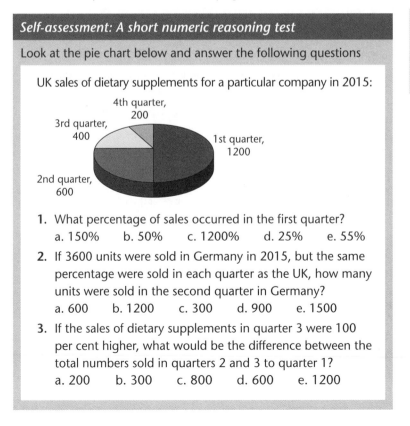

Self-assessment: A short numeric reasoning test

Look at the pie chart below and answer the following questions

UK sales of dietary supplements for a particular company in 2015:

4th quarter, 200

3rd quarter, 400

1st quarter, 1200

2nd quarter, 600

1. What percentage of sales occurred in the first quarter?
   a. 150%   b. 50%   c. 1200%   d. 25%   e. 55%

2. If 3600 units were sold in Germany in 2015, but the same percentage were sold in each quarter as the UK, how many units were sold in the second quarter in Germany?
   a. 600   b. 1200   c. 300   d. 900   e. 1500

3. If the sales of dietary supplements in quarter 3 were 100 per cent higher, what would be the difference between the total numbers sold in quarters 2 and 3 to quarter 1?
   a. 200   b. 300   c. 800   d. 600   e. 1200

Chapter 9

The answers:

1. b (50%)

How this is calculated:

- Total sales are 1200 + 600 + 400 + 200 = 2400.
- Sales in quarter 1 are 1200.
- Therefore, just by looking at the figures, you should be able to see that 1200 is half of 2400, i.e. 50%.

2. d (900)

How this is calculated:

- Total UK sales = 2400 (already established in question 1).
- Proportion of sales in quarter 2 = 600/2400 = 1/4.
- 1/4 of German sales = 3600/4 = 900.

3. a (200)

How this is calculated:

- Sales in quarter 3 = 400 (shown on the chart).
- 100% of 400 is 400 (you should just know this).
- Therefore, a sales increase of 100% = 400 + 400 = 800.
- Therefore, the sales totals for quarter 2 added to the adjusted figures for quarter 3 = 600 + 800 = 1400.
- Quarter 1 has sales figures of 1200; therefore, the difference is 1400 – 1200 = 200.

How to prepare

There are four ways you can substantially improve your performance:

1. Improve your basic maths and English skills Graduate-level verbal and numeric reasoning tests tend to assume applicants have roughly a GCSE level of competency in each of the subjects, but they often don't. Therefore, many applicants fail, not because they can't reason, but simply because they don't have the basic skills required. Ironically, most candidates would have had these skills at school but may well have let them slip at university because:

- These skills are often not tested on degree courses.
- Many academics don't mark students down for basic errors.

Therefore, before taking these tests, you should revise your maths and English skills. As far as the numeracy reasoning tests are concerned, you should be able to quickly and confidently manipulate basic number facts (such as multiplying by 10 or dividing by 2) and make accurate calculations in regard to the following elements, both mentally and on paper.

- Ratios
- Percentage increase or decrease
- Cost and sales analysis
- Rates and trends
- Currency conversions
- The four operations (addition, multiplication, subtraction and division)
- Fractions
- Information provided in tables, charts and figures.

Likewise, in literacy reasoning tests, you should be up to speed with respect to:

- Spelling
- Comprehension
- Synonyms
- Antonyms
- Grammar
- Punctuation
- The appropriate use of language

It may seem a bit much relearning all this just for a few tests, but it would be terrible if your career is held back just because you've forgotten a few basic processes. Besides, it will probably come rushing back to you as soon as you open a few revision guides. There are numerous maths and English GCSE books in the shops; you may also want to look up www.mathsrevision.net, which has well-structured courses, and/or www.bbc.co.uk/skillswise/english, which has specific English courses for adults.

2. Develop a strategy Once you've learned your stuff, there are two advantages to developing a robust strategy. Firstly, familiar routines will calm your nerves on the day, and secondly, you'll know what to do when you get stuck. This applies to the tests themselves and the individual questions. In terms of the tests, you should get used to the following:

- Your equipment: for example, your computer and calculator
- The location (if possible)
- Keeping abreast of the remaining time

- Devoting the appropriate time to each question
- Speedily checking your answers
- The order in which you like to answer the questions
- Moving on when you get stuck.

Decide whether you prefer to read the passages first and then the questions, or vice versa. For maths and abstract problems, it's wise to get to know your favourite problem-solving method for each type of question.

3. Practise Now you know what you're doing and how you're going to do it, it's time to have a go. The recruiters should provide a few practice questions and tell you where to find more. A large number of web-based organisations also offer similar tests for a small fee, and you can buy a large number of books on the subject. Your careers service may also be able to offer access to these guides, workshops and practice online sessions. For example, the University of Kent's website at www.kent.ac.uk/careers offers six practice verbal and numeric reasoning tests and numerous links to more.

4. Organise your day When the big day comes, you should relax and enjoy the challenge. Make sure you've eaten healthily, avoided alcohol and got some rest, as your brain works significantly better when it's fresh. If you're taking the tests online, choose the time of day when you're brightest. Most people work better in the mornings, but not everyone. Check that all your equipment is working and powered up, and make sure you understand how it works. Get some spare paper and your timepiece in position, and kick off.

You can find out more about assessment centres in *How to Succeed at Assessment Centres* (Houston, 2015).

Interviews

Most jobs and volunteering opportunities require an interview. Students and new graduates tend to find these direct interactions with employers quite challenging, but there are three key ways you can prepare.

Get used to meeting professionals

Find ways to meet influential people in a range of new social situations. This will gradually put you at ease in their company and help you perform more naturally when you're looking for a job. There are endless opportunities to meet professionals at university (and afterwards). For example, you could:

- Find voluntary/work roles where you can rub shoulders.
- Go out of your way to build new relationships during your voluntary/work roles.
- Attend careers events.
- Use your networks to arrange five-minute chats with people in the sector you're hoping to enter (see Chapter 3).

You can then practise your interview technique as you go for entry-level posts, and gradually improve as you move forward.

Learn what's involved

Interviews are designed to test your skills, commitment and knowledge. However, they are less of a theoretical exam than most people appreciate and more about seeing if you'll fit in. Therefore, you need to build rapport.

Prepare

As interviews tend to test the same attributes as applications, you should already have a good idea of what they're after and how you can prove your worth. If not, have a look back at the earlier sections of this chapter about researching vacancies. To prepare for the interview, you just need to get used to discussing these issues rather than just writing them down.

Questions on your skills (what you have to offer)

Most of the questions at each interview will test your relevant technical and transferable skills. Therefore, you should identify the skills required and learn your relevant attributes by rote. Once again, this involves memorising three specific ways you excel in each skill and providing a specific example.

> **Some typical skills-based questions**
>
> - Tell us about a time you worked in a team.
> - How do you change batteries on a CZ55?
> - Give an example of a time you negotiated a good price with a manufacturer?

If you prepare thoroughly in this way, then, on the day, all you'll have to do is figure out which specific skill is being tested in each question and convey your attributes accordingly. An example skills-based question and a good answer are shown below for an attribute required in the tutoring role shown earlier. As you can see, this example question is quite straightforward.

Skills-based question and answer:

Question: Can you please tell us how you inspire children in your maths lessons?

Answer: I'm really glad you asked me that because so many students are scared off by maths and lose their confidence, so I love to share my passion for the subject and engage children with the joy that can be found from finding solutions to interesting problems. ●————

Provide a really positive introduction so the interviewers can mentally prepare themselves for your answers and put themselves in a good position to listen.

I inspire students in three ways:

1. I demonstrate my genuine excitement, and this rubs off ●——— on the children.

2. I make sure my lessons are differentiated, so the outcomes ●—— are within everybody's grasp.

3. I praise and encourage success. ●———

Clearly outline the three traits you've revised (because this skill is listed in the personal specification).

For example, I recently helped a group of children with fractions at St Anthony's Primary. I first acquainted myself ●— with each child's recorded level of ability and the exercises he or she had already covered. I then introduced my lesson with a five-minute comedy sketch about sharing up sweets. This got the children in the mood. I then set a short exercise which reinforced their existing learning. ●———

Provide your prepared example which demonstrates the positive traits you've outlined.

For the main part of the lesson, I got the students to design a display for the classroom with everyday objects divided into fractions. In doing this, I was able to get each child to push his or her skill to the limit, advance the child's understanding and design a permanent reminder to show off to schoolmates, parents and the wider community.

As with application forms, use the STAR technique, i.e. give sparse detail about the situation and task but focus on what you actually did.

The display is still there today, and the children remain ●——— inspired.

Provide a short, positive ending.

All your questions won't be as obvious as the one above, but if you know your skills upside down and inside out, you should be able to wedge the specific attributes and examples you've memorised into almost any scenario. See below for how you could adapt your ability to inspire to fit some trickier questions.

Some possible questions and answers on how you inspire	
Straightforward questions	
● How do you get children motivated?	Here, you just need to recognise that 'motivate' means inspire, so just give the exact answer you've prepared.
● Why is it important to inspire children?	Adapt your introduction to use the word 'important', then provide your default answer (even though your skills and example haven't directly been mentioned).
Behavioural questions	
● Tell us when you've inspired your students to achieve.	Just give your stock answer, perhaps with a longer conclusion about what the children gained.
● When have you faced a challenge to get children excited?	Again, your stock answer can be given with a bit more in the introduction about why this was a challenge.
Situational questions	
● How would you inspire a child with maths?	Refocus your answer by referring to one particular child rather than the group in general.
● If you had to encourage more effort from children, how would you do it?	Adapt your introduction to focus on how inspiration is the best way to encourage students, and then go into your stock answer.

In the table above, you'll note that questions may not specifically mention one of the particular skills you've revised. This could mean the employer is asking about new skills altogether, in which case, you should still try to outline your attributes as best you can. However, it's more likely that these unfamiliar questions are actually still about the skills you've revised; they just haven't referred to them directly (e.g. the first question uses the word 'motivate' rather than 'inspire'). Therefore, before answering any strange questions, pause for a moment and try to identify exactly what the interviewer is after; also, don't feel awkward about asking for clarification.

Another key thing to note from the examples above is that most interview questions will not actually ask you directly *how* you perform particular skills to a high level or to *provide specific examples*, but you should always endeavour to get these elements into your answers, as they are the best way to prove your worth. Don't worry if you're just starting out in life, and your skills or examples are relatively undeveloped. Employers will take your inexperience into account.

The questions in the table have been divided into three common categories preferred by students and graduate employers, which are defined as follows:

- **Straightforward:** direct enquiries.
- **Behavioural:** queries about how you have demonstrated attributes in the past.
- **Situational:** questions about what you would do in a particular scenario.

Prepare for the different questions you may be asked on each skill by brainstorming all sorts of different angles and amending your answers appropriately. It can also help to get someone else to frame new questions for you so you can practise thinking on your feet. Try this in the activity below. You can complete the exercise right here or download it from the companion website at www.palgravecareerskills.com.

Self-assessment: Preparing for skills questions at interview

1. Identify a skill required in a post you're seeking.

2. List three ways you demonstrate this skill to a high level.

1.
2.
3.

3. Briefly outline a specific example.

4. Think of three possible questions relating to this skill, and outline how you could fit your specific attributes and example into your answer.

Possible questions	How you could answer
A straightforward question:	
A behavioural question:	
A situational question:	

Questions on your commitment (what drives you)

Your commitment is your passion and preparedness for the task in hand, and is as important as your skills. Therefore, employers tend to ask a whole range of questions about what you know about the job and why you want to come on board. Some examples are shown alongside.

The key to answering these questions is your ability to demonstrate that you've taken control of your career and have a genuine interest in the role. This, in turn, means you need to show that you've reflected on your skills, interests and motivations and have made appropriate decisions.

Don't worry if you're still not sure what you have to offer or where you want to go in life, but pass on any personal reflection you can. For example, you could back up your interest in a voluntary counselling role by explaining that you enjoy helping people and you want the chance to develop your listening skills for a later career in either teaching or law.

> ### Some typical commitment questions
>
> - Why have you applied?
> - What do you know about our organisation and competitors?
> - What attracts you to our sector?
> - How has this industry been affected by the recession?
> - Why have you applied for this job?
> - Why do you want to work at a small northern firm?
> - Why do you want to be a...? (Whatever the job is)
> - How does your degree relate to this position?

You can prepare for competency-based questions at each interview by reflecting as deeply as possible about these points:

- What you want to do in your career and why, in terms of your interests and motivations (even if these are still vague)
- What you've done so far to achieve your aims
- How your recent experiences have helped you progress
- What attracts you to the particular industry, sector, organisation and role
- How this opportunity will help you move on in your career.

Familiarise yourself with each of these issues before going to your interview, and you should be able to answer any competency-based questions. Try it now in the activity below. You can complete the exercise right here or download it from the companion website at www.palgravecareerskills.com.

Self-assessment: Preparing for competency questions

Find an interesting vacancy and answer the following questions.

1. What do you want to do in your career and why?

2. What have you done so far to achieve your aims (e.g., choosing a particular degree, volunteering or paid work)?

3. How have each of your recent experiences helped you move towards your goal?

   Experience 1:

   Experience 2:

   Experience 3:

   Experience 4:

4. What attracts you to the specific . . .

   Industry?

   Sector?

   Organisation?

   Role?

5. How will this opportunity help you move on?

An example of a good answer to a common commitment–based question is shown below. This example is again related to the maths tutoring role outlined earlier in the chapter.

A commitment-based question and answer

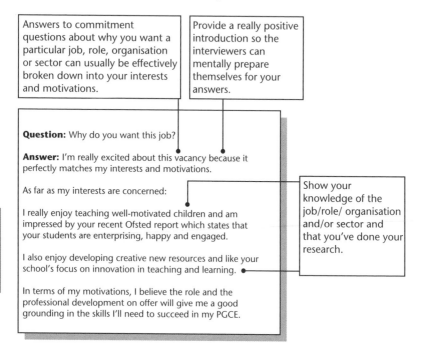

Answers to commitment questions about why you want a particular job, role, organisation or sector can usually be effectively broken down into your interests and motivations.

Provide a really positive introduction so the interviewers can mentally prepare themselves for your answers.

Question: Why do you want this job?

Answer: I'm really excited about this vacancy because it perfectly matches my interests and motivations.

As far as my interests are concerned:

I really enjoy teaching well-motivated children and am impressed by your recent Ofsted report which states that your students are enterprising, happy and engaged.

I also enjoy developing creative new resources and like your school's focus on innovation in teaching and learning.

In terms of my motivations, I believe the role and the professional development on offer will give me a good grounding in the skills I'll need to succeed in my PGCE.

Show your knowledge of the job/role/ organisation and/or sector and that you've done your research.

Questions on your knowledge (what you know) Questions in this category are rare because there are better ways to test your technical capabilities and knowledge. Example questions could be something like 'What is a hydrofoil?' or 'What are the guiding principles of the scouting movement?' You can prepare for these questions by making sure you understand the role you're going for, keeping up with current practices and issues in your chosen sector and learning the jargon.

Your body language

Because interviews are such a personal interaction, it's really important that you give a good impression. Here are some tips:

- Remain calm (aim to get to the venue at least an hour before kick-off and go for a walk so you're energised but relaxed; enter the venue with about 10 minutes to spare).

- Be courteous with everyone you meet.
- Shake hands firmly (if they initiate such a welcome).
- Smile.
- Walk upright with confidence.
- Sit up straight.
- Look into the interviewers' eyes while they're asking their questions, and scan their faces as you answer.
- Address the interviewers using their names.

A typical interview structure

Interviews often adopt the following format:

1. **The interviewers will invite you in and say hello:** Be pleasant, walk purposefully, hold your head up high and smile at everyone in the room.
2. **The interviewer/panel will introduce themselves:** It's a good idea to respond to each interviewer in turn, saying something like 'Hello John' (if his name is John). This will help you remember the interviewers' names so you can refer to them by name later (a good tactic).
3. **The interviewer(s) will ask a simple warm-up question:** They usually ask a 'throw-away' question to help you get warmed up, such as 'Did you find us okay?' This is your opportunity to demonstrate your preparedness by saying something like: 'Yes, I left early so I'd be able to get here on time, and looked around the gallery whilst I waited' [for a job in a museum].

4. **Question 1: Some sort of variant of 'Why do you want this role/ Why do you want to work for us?'** This is a common initial question. Prove your commitment as advised throughout this chapter.

5. **Question 2: Some sort of variant of 'What have you got to offer/Why should we hire you?'** Briefly outline how you perform the top three skills required (as advised throughout this chapter). Make sure you don't mix up your answers to questions 1 and 2, in whatever order they're asked. One refers to why you want the job, and the other to what you have to offer (two different things).

6. **Questions 3–7: Various other questions related to the skills, commitment and knowledge required:** Take your time to clarify what's being asked, and systematically demonstrate your attributes as per your homework. Make sure you give specific examples, whether or not they're requested.

7. **Penultimate question: 'What are your weaknesses?'** One tactic here is to outline a relatively unimportant weakness that's not so relevant to the specific role. However, you should also state what you've done to address the weakness and comment on how your actions have actually given you relative strengths in other areas that are relevant.

8. **A typical ultimate question is 'Do you have any questions for us?'** This is your chance to find out anything about the role you've yet to discover and impress the panel with your research. For example:

> 𝕘𝕘 I notice that, during my training, I will be given the opportunity to work in a range of sectors of the business. Please, could you outline what these are? 𝕛𝕛

You should avoid overly grand questions about the organisation in general (as these will almost certainly not be relevant to your post) or queries at this stage about details such as your salary or annual leave.

Phil Nicholls, EMERGE IT

We are an IT solution provider and support organisation, and need people who can relate well with our customers. Therefore, the personality aspects of roles are often more important than the technical, as we are able to train the technical requirements, but not the personality traits.

Consequently, our recruitment practices are heavily designed to test candidates' relevant values and personal capabilities such as their ability to go the extra mile, communicate and persevere. We use a number of different strategies to clearly ascertain these intrinsic capabilities. These include CVs, personality tests, interviews (including a logic-based question which forces applicants to think on their feet), group exercises and a presentation.

As we are testing very personal attributes, much of this process is inherently subjective, but we take the time to look at candidates' performance in the round, not just their performance at one particular stage of the application process. We recently found two new interns through Step; both worked out really well and have accepted permanent offers to work full-time.

Presentations

What they're all about

Employers often ask candidates to make short presentations, either on their own or as part of a group. They will give you the topic either in advance or on the day, and it may or may not be directly related to the role. Many people find it very challenging to perform in this way, especially when they're just starting out, but there are a number of things you can do to impress.

Say something worth saying

Research your audience, and choose a topic and viewpoint that they will genuinely find interesting. For example, if you're talking to primary school teachers, in 2015, you may want to focus on the imminent eradication of educational levels.

Of course, if the topic is chosen for you, you have limited scope in this regard, but take some time to figure out why the organisation has chosen that particular issue, and speak to their motivations. For example:

- If they want to hear about you, then they clearly want you to demonstrate how you meet the selection criteria.
- If they want you to make a presentation about a particular current affair, they probably want to hear your take on how it affects their particular industry and organisation.

Chapter 9

Target the make-up of your audience

Every group of people is unique, and you should therefore amend your delivery accordingly. This involves researching each organisation and adapting every aspect of your talk from the words you use, to the statistics, your level of interaction and your props. However, don't let this consideration stultify your natural style, as you should always be dynamic and engaging. For example, new employees at a marketing firm will probably prefer a more active approach than underwriters at Lloyds, and academics may want to hear a greater level of in-depth analysis than lifesavers at the beach.

Present!

Presentations are not just about standing there and reading out your notes as quickly as possible. You have to perform. Face the audience, interact naturally with other presenters, look people in the eye, talk directly, modulate your voice, smile, laugh, and speak slowly and audibly with absolute clarity.

Also, be careful you don't start to gradually speed up as you get further into your talk, because your adrenaline will probably be telling you to go at a hundred miles per hour. You should also use simple words, short sentences and avoid jargon. And stick to the point: Always remember that most good presentations are short and sweet. Plus, whatever you do, stick to the time limit.

Some people feel the need to bring in cue cards in case they forget their lines, but this can be very dangerous because you'll probably panic at some point, look down at what you've written and start reading. Then, because you can't think of anything but the words on your notes, you won't be able to get back into stride. You can avoid this calamity by:

- Keeping your presentations short.
- Being well prepared (i.e. practising over and over again).
- Using cue cards with single words to signify new points rather than writing out your full text (or even better still, using pictures).

Interact

One good way to wake up your audience in your presentations is involving them from the start. The easiest way to do this is to ask questions. You can increase your chances of getting answers by making your queries easy and straightforward and/or targeting them at particular people. Here are some suggestions for other creative ways of involving your audience:

- Ask them to discuss certain issues with a partner, and then provide feedback in some way.
- Get them to complete simple tasks (either mentally or manually).
- Incorporate competitions with prizes, such as games of jargon bingo where you give them cards of subject-related clichés they have to listen out for.

Use props and visual aids

Your body Visual aids are a great tool to engage people and, of course, the biggest prop you'll have in most talks is your own body. Listed here are some ways to maximise your impact:

- Face the audience, and never read from the slides (the audience can read for themselves).

- Avoid standing behind a podium unless you've been told to do so or it's absolutely necessary for some reason (mice can usually be moved nowadays).

- Don't stand in front of your other visual aids (e.g. your slides).

- Move around at key points (but not all the time).

- Use your arms (and any other parts of your body) to exaggerate your points.

- In group presentations, make sure the handovers are smooth and you maintain pace. Also, if possible, avoid just moving on from one person to another in a sequence – get each member to jump in and out and interact in more interesting ways.

Other objects Any other big, shiny objects which are related to your talk can also add value, especially if you produce them unexpectedly. For example, if you're talking about CVs, you may literally want to bring in a long, boring autobiography to show the audience what to avoid.

Your slides Posters and PowerPoint® slides are often poorly designed. In particular, they can be difficult to read or jam-packed with too much information. You can avoid these common mistakes by using:

- A large font size (above size 30 in PowerPoint).

- As few words as possible. For example, on PowerPoint, limit each slide to about 20.

- As few slides as possible – six should do for a 20-minute talk; otherwise, they take over, and you'll end up just rushing through them without taking the time to properly address any of the issues.

- Colour and big pictures, but don't get carried away, as too many 'bells and whistles' can be distracting.

- Simple graphs and diagrams.

- Elements which require the most basic software. For example, video and websites that look brilliant on your computer at home may not be supported at the venue, and you'll look disorganised.

These points are illustrated on the example slide shown below.

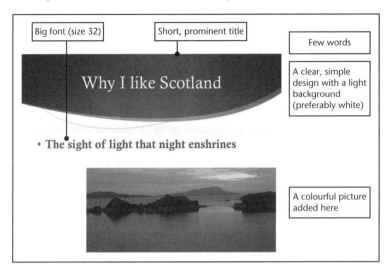

Have a look at Guy Kawasaki's video at www.youtube.com for a frank and funny outline of a good presentation technique called '10/20/30'.

Focusing on your structure

Good structure is absolutely vital to effective presentations. This is because the audience can very easily get lost in the maze of information. With books, the Internet or a video, people can pause, look back over what's been covered and see where each part fits the whole. However, in your talks they don't have this luxury, so you have to continually keep them up to speed. In the words of Dale Carnegie: 'Tell the audience what you're going to say, say it; then tell them what you've said.' In practice, this means you should:

- Start your presentation with a short outline of what you're going to cover
- Raise your first point
- Refer back to your outline
- Raise your second point
- Refer back to your outline
- Raise your third point
- Summarise.

This focus on structure is crucial – even if your talks are only five minutes long!

One way you can help your audience is to keep your plans for talks permanently on display and refer back to them on a regular basis. For example, you could do this on a separate poster (but make sure the text is large enough for people at the back of the room).

Once you've introduced what you're going to say, divide the remainder of your talk into as few key points as possible – certainly, no more than three. Devote a new slide or poster to each one, but don't try to cram in everything you want to convey. Your slides should be visual aids, not reading material. In fact, some of the best presentations have no words at all, just simple pictures, diagrams or graphs. If you need to impart a great deal of information, give your audience a handout, but not until you've finished or they'll just sit there reading it whilst you're on stage.

Expand on each point, but again, keep it simple. Stick to the absolutely key information.

Finally, include a poster or slide to briefly summarise what you've covered, or refer back to the key points which you've displayed throughout. Easy!

Practise

As with any other skill, practice makes perfect, but don't wait until your first interview to get into the swing of things. Get involved in public speaking and presentations at university and all other spheres of your life. However, don't fall into bad habits, as poor student presentations are often tolerated and not criticised.

When it comes to preparing for specific talks:

- Familiarise yourself with the subject matter.
- Take a great deal of care with your visual aids.
- Go over and over again what you're going to say, how you're going to say it and where you're going to stand.
- Get your timings second-perfect.

Don't just go through the presentations in your head – practise in a room or hall similar to the one where you're going to perform.

Dealing with nerves

There are a number of strategies you can employ to minimise your nerves:

- Prepare assiduously.
- Use simple IT because if technology can go wrong, it will.
- Be totally familiar with your subject.
- Don't say much – just the key point(s) will do. Therefore, you should be able to remember your whole talk by heart.
- Avoid too many statistics and difficult technical concepts/ definitions.
- Eat sensibly beforehand.
- Spend some time in quiet contemplation before you step onto the stage, and control your breathing.
- Take it easy – if you make light of your small mistakes, then so will the panel.

Group exercises

These are activities in which you will be put into a group of six or seven people to solve a practical problem or discuss a current issue and present your findings. The issues involved are not usually too taxing, as employers are really testing your ability to work collaboratively and creatively when you're under pressure. Prepare for these activities by:

- Identifying how you work well in teams.
- Exploring how you can demonstrate these attributes to the assessors on the day.

For example, if you're good at encouraging people, you could focus on impressing assessors by praising colleagues and introducing shy people into the discussion (especially when the assessors hover over you with flipcharts in hand).

Ben Short, Recruitment and Resourcing Consultant

My main tip for assessment centres in general is to be prepared. If you have a presentation topic make sure you have fully answered the question; an interview, make sure you know the company (even what that specific site you are at does); and for group exercises, make sure you contribute – but don't waffle.

It is amazing how many people sit in silence or just talk for the sake of talking. Not everything said is worth saying, and not everything worth saying gets said.

Presentation: If I ask you to tell me how your project relates to our company, I am looking at your understanding of how your skill set matches our business. Ignoring this part of the question completely questions your ability to follow instructions, as well as loses you a large chunk of the potential scores for the task.

What to do now

Get used to researching what employers are after, objectively appraising your abilities and promoting yourself. It can take some time to develop these skills, but once you know what you're doing, you'll never forget, and all sorts of doors will open up.

Happy job-hunting!

Notes

Chapter 01

1. See the website of the Higher Education Statistics Agency at www.hesa.ac.uk/stats.
2. See Kent University Careers Advisory Service website at www.kent.ac.uk/careers/sk/top-ten-skills.htm.

Chapter 03

1. The Oxford Concise Dictionary.
2. 'Chain Links', by Frigyes Karinthy.
3. See Jobvite's 2014 Social Recruiting Survey on www.jobvite.com.
4. www.ceb.shl.com/assets/GATR_2013_US.pdf
5. www.statista.com
6. www.bbc.com/capital/story/20150505-land-a-job-in-140-characters-or-less
7. See: 'The Global Trends That Will Shape Recruiting in 2015' on https://www.linkedin.com
8. www.bc.edu

Chapter 04

1. See the 'Citizens Survey' at www.discover.ukdataservice.ac.uk
2. www.timebank.org.uk/key-facts

Chapter 05

1. www.endsleigh.co.uk
2. Franklin, B. (1817) *The complete works of Benjamin Franklin*. New York: G.P. Putman's Sons.

Chapter 06

1. www.dictionary.cambridge.org
2. www.highfliers.co.uk/download/GMReport14.pdf
3. www.gov.uk/government/uploads/system/uploads/attachment_
   data/file/367461/State_of_the_Nation_-_summary_document.pdf
4. www.highfliers.co.uk
5. www.asetonline.org

Chapter 07

1. www.gapadvice.org

Chapter 08

1. See 'Benefits of Work Placements' at http://intranet.londonmet.
   ac.uk/studentservices
2. Einstein, A. (2011) *Letters to Solovine: 1906–1955*. New York:
   Philosophical Library/Open Road.

References

Houston, K. (2015) *How to Succeed at Assessment Centres*. London: Palgrave.

Kelly, M. (2015) *Social Media for your Student and Graduate Job Search*. London: Palgrave.

Rook, S. (2013) *The Graduate Career Guidebook*. London: Palgrave.

Index